HEAVENVISION

Glimpses into Glory

TERRY JAMES
WITH ANGIE PETERS

First printing: December 2012

For information contact:
Icon Publishing
Customer Service: +1 877 887 0222
P.O. Box 2180
Noble, OK 73068

ISBN: 978-1-62022-040-5

Cover by Nick Peters of Benton, Arkansas
Interior by Brent Spurlock of Green Forest, Arkansas

Please visit our website for other great titles:
www.iconpublishinggroup.com

DEDICATION

Dedicated to my mother, Kathleen McDuffie James Basse

and to my aunt, Betty Jane McDuffie-Dunn

Life is hard—but God is good,
and Heaven is real.

–Billy Graham[1]

TABLE OF CONTENTS

Preface
by Angie Peters

Imagine what it would be like to win a round-trip ticket to Heaven. That's what happened to the apostle Paul when he was "caught up into paradise" (2 Corinthians 12:2–4). He reports the following:

> I know a man in Christ who fourteen years ago—whether in the body I do not know, or out of the body I do not know, God knows—such a man was caught up to the third heaven. And I know how such a man—whether in the body or apart from the body I do not know, God knows—was caught up into Paradise and heard inexpressible words, which a man is not permitted to speak.

As we might guess, what Paul saw and heard was so magnificent and hard to understand that not only was he unable to describe the experience, but also, for reasons he doesn't say, he was forbidden to try.

Some Bible scholars take the restriction on Paul as a sort of divine gag order, saying it means that speaking of such glimpses into glory is taboo. If Paul wasn't allowed to relate the details of his heavenly experience, they say, no one should be allowed to do so.

Yet Paul certainly wasn't the only person in Scripture for whom the blinds on the windows of Heaven were raised, at least for a time. There's also Stephen, as well as the prophets Ezekiel and John. Note that when the latter two were given glimpses into glory, they weren't told to be silent. Quite the opposite: They were instructed to relate in great detail the dazzling particulars of what they saw, heard, and experienced. "But you shall speak My words to them whether they listen or not," the Lord God told Ezekiel (Ezekiel 2:7). And, "Therefore write the things which you have seen, and the things which are, and the things which will take place after these things" (Revelation 1:19), the Risen Christ directed John. No gag orders there.

Many other people through the ages—not just biblical martyrs, super saints, and wizened prophets, but regular Joes and ordinary Janes—have been allowed brief glimpses into glory as they teetered on the boundary between Earth and eternity. Books like *90 Minutes in Heaven* and *Heaven Is for Real* have gotten the word out about the results of many of these experiences, as has the TV series *Beyond and Back* on A&E Networks' Biography Channel, which debuted in the fall of 2010 with the highest ratings of any new show ever to premiere on the BIO channel to that point. Apparently, things having to do with what comes after this life—and with what Heaven might hold—intrigue just about everyone…including me. As one who has loved Jesus for as long as I can remember, there's never been any doubt in my mind about my after-life destination. I know I'm going to Heaven when I die! The only questions I've had have been about the details of that place…if you can even really call it a "place."

So, once I was assured that Terry James, my close friend, mentor, and writing partner for nearly twenty years, was out of the woods after his heart attack, I couldn't wait to hear what, if anything, he had experienced while his heartbeat had been still and silent those three times. And he couldn't wait to tell me. He confirmed from his hospital bed that Good Friday afternoon in the cardiovascular intensive care unit of the hospital in our small town that even though "things which eye has not seen and ear has not heard, and which have not entered the heart of man" (1 Corinthians 2:9) is the operative truth, God does allow a number of His children a limited look at certain "things." What the Lord chooses to share through the near-death experiences He allows some people may be hard to make sense of, to a certain degree, but we can't overlook the intriguing promise of 1 Corinthians 2:10: When the Holy Spirit is allowed to serve as the translator, He makes spiritual matters understandable. (That's with one limitation: only to those who love Him; see 1 Corinthians 2:11.) I know Terry well, and if there were ever a person to rely on the appropriate translator for spiritual matters, he's our guy.

What the Holy Spirit allowed my blind pal to see (with perfect focus and in vivid colors, I was thrilled to learn), hear, feel, and understand during his glimpses into glory is a big part of what we'll be sharing throughout the pages of this book. I don't have anything as dramatic as a peek into the windows of Paradise to add to his material, but I'm honored beyond words to be invited to join him in looking at how his story and the in-between-life-and-death accounts of many others affirm the promises the Lord has given us about Heaven in His Word.

Interestingly, what we found in our research is that while every individual's near-death story is unique, many common threads are woven through their narratives. Experiences like feeling a heightened sense of awareness, recognizing loved ones, and enjoying perfect health and well being are just a few of the similarities that crop up time and time again in the accounts of personal brushes with death. Even more intriguing is the fact that many of these common experiences are directly linked to information the Bible gives us about Heaven. Do I view these personal accounts as some sort of proof that what the Bible says about Heaven is true? Absolutely not. The truth of God's Word needs no proof. Here's how I see them: Just as God might use things like a stunning sunset, a baby's birth, a restored relation-ship, a friend's embrace, or an answered prayer to reinforce my belief that He's at work in each of us in a very personal way in our day-to-day lives on Earth, I believe He uses these life-after-life glimpses to fortify my faith in Him, giving at least some shape and form to the hope I have in looking forward to the life He's preparing for me to live…even long after I take my last breath. It is my prayer that He will do the same for you.

ACKNOWLEDGMENTS

HeavenVision: Glimpses into Glory is a part of my life come to pass only because the Lord of Creation determined that I return through death's portal to present the story. So, the first and foremost acknowledgment of thanksgiving is to the Lord Jesus Christ, who made its telling possible.

Jesus alone holds the keys to death and Hell. Thankfully, He also holds the keys to the magnificent heavenly abode—the Father's house. The Son of God died and arose from the dead, and now all who believe in Him can one day make that journey into the glorious land where He has prepared incomprehensibly beautiful dwelling places for God's family.

However, there are also many others who deserve acknowledgment for their parts in this amazing trip to Heaven and back.

My mother, Kathleen James Basse, to whom I've dedicated this book, is the person who saw to it that I was put in front of the throne of God at every opportunity in order that I learn about the greatest story ever told, up close and personal. My eternal gratitude to you, Mom.

My dad, Bill James, who is now with the Lord, although quiet in his way of shaping the lives of my brother and me, also deserves Robin's and my heartfelt thanks. I'm sure he will receive rewards at the proper moment in the hereafter.

To my wife, Margaret, and our sons, Terry, Jr., and Nathan, my love and thanks for always being there for me—in sickness and in health.

To Angie Peters, my coauthor, who has masterfully written for and shaped this volume as no one else could, and who has meant so very much to me personally and professionally for twenty years, my most profound love and thanks.

To Dana Neel, another of my extended family members and honorary daughters, my love and many thanks for the great research provided in the writing of this book and my other books.

To Jeanie Hedges; Todd Strandberg, my partner in and founder of www.raptureready.com; Mike Hile; and Kit Olsen—all of whom I also consider my extended family, my love and thanks for their warm, nurturing friendship.

May the Lord bless all who read the things written herein. It is a truly astonishing testimony—not to my life accomplishments, but to the reality of God's mercy, grace, and love.

–Terry James

BEFORE MY FIRST LAST HEARTBEAT

February 25, 2011, my notes show.

I was sitting at my desk thinking about a promise I had made to my mother. I'd been telling her for months that I would write a book on Heaven.

She had read one particular book about the subject that she really loved, and had passed it on to a number of friends, including my aunt—Auntie Bet (for Bettie), as I've always called her. My aunt read it quickly—it was very short—and now I had both Mom and her sister on my case to write something on Heaven. I've been writing books about nothing but end-time events and Bible prophecy for many years, so I guess they believed it was about time for me to tackle a different topic. Maybe they wanted to see me focus on "after-time" events instead of "end-of-time" events for a change.

More importantly, I had been feeling a nudge from the Holy Spirit to begin the project. So, the planning was launched that icy winter morning, a steady stream of notes being scribbled onto a computer document over the following days and weeks. (Since the early 1990s, my blindness has prevented me from using the much-beloved yellow legal pad and black Flair pen to jot down project notes; I now scrawl and jot by typing on my keyboard with a JAWS [Jobs Accessible Word System] voice-synthesis program that reads to me every letter, punctuation mark, sentence, paragraph, or complete document that I type or open.)

Mom had done as she promised—recorded the little book about Heaven on cassette tape for me. As I listened to the familiar lilt and timbre of her sweet southern voice, bits and pieces of what she was reading gave inspiration and impetus to a number of thoughts, but primarily to one: I would approach my book on Heaven from the perspective of some who claimed to have had near-death experiences. These would have to be documented clinical deaths, I decided, of people who had told what they had seen, heard, and felt when they had been on the brink of eternity.

Thousands of other thoughts about how to approach the writing went through my mind as well while I brainstormed for the book project, with one of the ideas even compelling me to chuckle and whisper to myself while I paced about my study and the rest of the house: "Boy! Wouldn't it be something to have one of those near-death experiences?" I wondered aloud. "Wouldn't that be something? Would *that* ever add to the book!"

What if I just suddenly dropped right here, died a clinical death, then snapped out of it after a heavenly experience the Lord let me survive? Notice that I never thought: *What if it was a car accident and I was horribly mangled?* That's what happened in Don Piper's near-death experience recounted in his best-selling book, *90 Minutes in Heaven.* I hadn't even yet read his account. The "what if?" was just: drop, have the experience, and survive to write about it.

Be careful what you wish for, as they say.

On Good Friday—April 22—of 2011, I was given the kind of firsthand experience about which I had been, to some extent, fantasizing. I received a personal trip across that great divide between earthly life and life after death to get a glimpse of the "other" side. My journey motivated me to return with even more gusto to my research into what is known about life after life, and to realistically consider Heaven's enthralling possibilities.

———•◦•———

An evangelist I once heard describe his vision-visit to Heaven told how he was one on one with Jesus somewhere in glory. Jesus was weeping, the evangelist said, while telling him all about how saddened He was over sinners who will have to spend eternity apart from the glorious abode of God. The evangelist and the Lord were, it seems, like a couple of close chums. To hear this man talk, it was almost like he was comforting Jesus.

The man supposedly was taken there—to Heaven—one evening while he was preparing to preach a service. He was back and again in the present with time left over to shower and get dressed, according to the story. There was no near-death experience—just a whisking away as the man fell unconscious.

When I started thinking about writing this book, these kinds of stories troubled me. For example, in the above account, how could the Lord of all creation be weeping, when Jesus' very words say that all tears will be wiped away in Heaven (Revelation 21:4)? That just doesn't add up. While I don't mean to imply the above-mentioned evangelist was one of Satan's minions, the truth is, the spiritual world includes evil as well as good, and it is the goal of the forces of darkness and wickedness spoken of in Ephesians 6:12 to distort God's truth. As Mark Hitchcock points out in his book, *55 Answers to Questions about Life after Death:*

> The Bible says that since God is light, Satan disguises himself as an angel of light to deceive the unsuspecting (2 Corinthians 11:14). Wouldn't it be expected that the great deceiver would try to lead people who don't know Christ to believe that when they die everything will be great? Doesn't it make sense that Satan would seek to convince men and women that one's relationship to Christ has no bearing on seeing the great light and entering heaven? This is Satan's greatest lie. We shouldn't be surprised that he would use it in an experience like an NDE [near-death experience] to give some people false security about their eternal destiny.[2]

So, with a keen awareness of the gravity of the topic of Heaven, I decided from the start to handle it with extreme care. Separating genuine near-death experiences from fabrications and legitimate visions from fables would have to be a constant goal, as would keeping God's Word at the very center of the work—all the while praying for His lead in forming each thought and composing each sentence. I didn't want to give critics any kind of a foothold. And, believe me, considering that things to do with the afterlife are such hot-button topics, I knew there would be critics—even among those in my circle of friends and colleagues, and among those whose teachings I follow.

For example, listening to one of my favorite Bible teachers one recent Saturday morning, I heard him say, "We should be sweet to those…who think they've had experiences like dying and coming back." He went on to say, in so many words, that these episodes were likely the brain playing tricks, much like dreams. He dismissed any such accounts as well-intentioned, even genuinely believed, by the ones who dream them—but held that they were strictly the result of a brain glitch produced by lack of oxygen or other physiological activity.

It was the late Dr. J. Vernon McGee answering a question many years ago on his radio program that is as good a teaching tool today as it was in the days when he was alive. Anyone who thinks to disagree with this wise, old saint should reconsider. So I did. But I concluded that there's no other way to say it: Dr. McGee was wrong. This great man of God was—in this matter—pardon the pun, *dead* wrong.

At one time I would've agreed almost entirely with his assessment. I'm very strongly theologically bent in a direction away from ecstatic experiences of any sort. These have too often been used to bring emotionalism into Bible teaching that is backed by no Holy Spirit influence whatsoever.

Here's an example I've used a number of times to debunk such emotional fable-fashioning:

A pastor and executive head of a regional Christian television network tells of the death of a "dear Christian brother" whose body lay in its casket in a mortuary for viewing. As the story goes, a high-powered evangelist was in town to conduct services for the CEO's church.

They took the preacher to the place of viewing, and he stood over the dearly departed for a moment before saying: "This dear brother isn't meant to be dead." He grabbed the corpse after lifting the closed half of the coffin lid, dragged the body from its resting place, and sat it up against the wall in the sitting-up position, legs straight out.

The evangelist stood back, glared downward at the embalmed dead man, and declared: "In the name of Jesus, I command you to get up and walk!"

According to the pastor, the body just slumped over with its stiff shoulder on the carpet.

Again, the evangelist reached down and placed the corpse with its back to the wall. And again, he said: "I command you, in the name of Jesus, get up and walk!"

The body slumped to the carpet.

Once more, the now-agitated evangelist put the body against the wall and shouted mightily: "In the name of Jesus, I command you to get up and walk!"

This time, the pastor/CEO said the corpse stood to its feet and walked out of the viewing room. Where the corpse walked, or where the now-walking-around dead man is today, has never been stated.

I've never heard anyone in the huge congregation that the man pastors ever question this account.

Neither *Tales from the Crypt* nor any other forum that tells of the macabre can top that one, in my estimation. I'm tempted to say that the pastor was embellishing for the sake of making a point, although I don't remember his point. Who could remember any of a sermon's objectives after hearing such a thing?

I'm also tempted to say that the pastor remembered the story and just got the details mixed up. But no. Jesus said: "It is appointed for men to die once and after this comes judgment" (Hebrews 9:27). If the man had truly been raised from the dead, he would have made medical history and science would be all over the case. If this gentleman—the evangelist—could raise the dead (especially a dead person who is embalmed), we would be hearing about it from mainstream journalists who would be clamoring for interviews with the "miracle worker." Such a man could not remain unknown. Jesus of Nazareth did just such miracles, and His name is known the world over and from generation to generation. As a matter of fact, His name, the Bible says, is above every name.

As I thought, then, about how to go about writing a book like this while distancing myself from such sensationalism, I couldn't help but wonder how people would assess my own vision, my clinical-death visit to wherever, in their truth meters. As a stodgy Baptist type for most of my sixty-eight years (my age at the time of my clinical deaths), dreams and visions have been as far from my theological bent as one might imagine. But I kept coming back to the truth: I experienced what I experienced, and I saw what I saw—with the most vivid eyesight possible (and me a totally blind person)! The Lord is my witness! And, Saline Memorial Hospital in Benton, Arkansas, has on file the records of that Good Friday, April 22, 2011, so the proof of my medical condition is there for anyone to check. I will gladly grant permission to release my medical record of that day.

My heart stopped working three times, and I was within ten seconds, according to the interventional cardiologist, of being beyond resuscitation. The defibrillator paddles were used each time to restart my heart.

When my heartbeat went silent, I didn't see Jesus or talk with Him. I didn't see the glorious city, Heaven. But what I did see was spectacular, and it made me totally unaware of ever having been anywhere else. So, rather than tell you that I know what Heaven looks like, which I can't, I will, over the course of these pages, tell you the things I did see, and will confide what I believe the Holy Spirit has shown me is wrapped up in the glimpse I was given.

But I won't just zero in on what happened to me. As I planned from the beginning—long before my own "glimpse into glory"— I would also like for us to examine what many others who claim to have had visions of the heavenly realm say they've seen and heard. My close friend and colleague, Angie Peters, and I have worked together to see how some of these accounts fit as God wills within the framework of His Holy Word.

This much I can say with certainty, even from the limited perspective I was granted during my brief experience: Heaven is magnificent far beyond anything the most eloquent narrative by the greatest of novelists could ever begin to express.

Chapter One

AWAKE!

"Awake, sleeper, And arise from the dead, And Christ will shine on you" (Ephesians 5:14).

TERRY JAMES—They beckoned to me. A throng of cheering, brightly smiling, laughter-filled young men and women, their faces radiant with the glowing health of youth, wanted me to join them. I had never been more at peace, absolute calm surrounding me…within me. This was life at its apex, and I moved forward, my desire to be with them as powerful as their allure.

A vividly colorful ambience generated by their love was overwhelming—like the sun's radiance that warms to the very core. Momentarily I would be with them, a part of them. Nothing else entered my mind—not questions of where I was, not thinking about where I had been. I was here. This was real, and the reality was all-embracing.

The young faces beamed with that shimmering glow, their eyes on me, their love gently tugging me toward them. Retrospectively, I longed to join them. I wanted to be a part of them more than anything I can remember ever wanting.

I say "retrospectively," because at that moment I had no memories: no thought of the past, the future, or anything else—just the desire to merge with this reality.

Darkness and confusion began engulfing me, then, and I wondered what was happening. I remember thinking, I don't want to leave this place.

———•———

"I just hit him with the paddles!" I heard someone say. I was back on the table, my mind returning.

"Hit me with the paddles?" I remember asking.

"Your heart stopped," the young man said, feverishly working over me as I lay stretched out on the gurney.

It was my first of three trips to…? Only God knows where.

———•———

I've worked out regularly since 1979, the year I could no longer see well enough to work in the corporate world. I had previously served as director of public relations in several companies, and was required to carry out a demanding schedule in that capacity. But as my eyesight had closed in peripherally so that I was no longer able to drive, travel out of town, and meet other obligations, I was forced to step out of the career I had poured my time and energy into for nine years to that point. I went on to work as an independent consultant in the advertising/public relations field for another twelve years. "Frustrated" is one of the many feelings I experienced over my new circumstances, so I decided to throw my frustration into working out at least four times a week. This has been my routine ever since.

As I mentioned earlier, it was Good Friday, April 22, 2011. At 1:30 or so in the afternoon, I was just completing my workout. I had done the weight lifting, the push-ups, and the sit-ups in the Body by Jake crunch machine. I had worked out on the rowing machine with the heavy weights and finished up my miles on the treadmill. And finally, my work on the recumbent bike—the last exercise as part of the cool down—was done when I began to feel a burning behind my sternum. It worsened by the second, so I stood and tried to walk off the pain.

I thought it was just a severe case of indigestion, although I had never experienced heartburn that bad. The pain increased and pressure built within my chest as if tremendous gas were pressing against the sternum. I found it harder and harder to breathe, and I was becoming clammy while I continued to try to walk off the burning sensation.

Finally, I plopped my six-foot frame into my recliner and told my wife, Margaret, "You'd better call 911. This is getting worse."

She knew that for me to give such an instruction meant something was definitely wrong. Calling for an ambulance for myself was the last thing I would do.

It almost was.

The paramedics arrived in about ten minutes. I was still on the recliner, trying to catch my breath. The pain was intensifying.

"I can't find a pulse," one of the guys said to another. The second medic came to check my wrist, then my neck. He couldn't find a pulse, either.

I was thinking, *No pulse. That means you're dead, doesn't it?*

Meanwhile, Margaret had answered the phone. It was my friend Mike calling to talk. I heard her telling him: "He's having some problems breathing or something. They're checking him." I know that Mike, when he got off the phone, immediately began praying for me, then he let others know so they could pray, too.

One of the medics asked if I could walk to the gurney just outside, because it would be quicker and easier than having to bring it in and take me out the door. I managed to do so, even without a pulse, I guess, because soon I was strapped onto the gurney and in the back of the van.

The pain was building, then subsiding, only to build again, while my sternum felt as if it would give way to the tremendous pressure building beneath. One of the medics had me open my mouth, and he put something liquid beneath my tongue.

"Is that digitalis?" I remember asking. "Nitroglycerin," he said, working feverishly on and around me.

I heard him identify himself on a phone, then say: "I think we have a coronary in progress."

A coronary? A heart attack! Me, of all people?

I felt every bump in the streets, thinking that ambulances sure aren't made for the patients' comfortable ride. Such foolish thoughts while one is having...a coronary.

The hospital is two miles away from my home, at most. Soon we stopped, and the medics were rushing around me. The pain was excruciating while they opened the vehicle's back doors and began pulling the gurney, with me on it, through the opening.

I heard the *blip,* then. It sounded exactly like the chime sometimes made when the computer goes from one web link to another.

TERRY JAMES—Instantly, I was looking at the large group of beautiful, young people I described at the beginning of this chapter—men and women who had all eyes on me. None was more than thirty years of age. They had their hands in the air, cheering. They motioned for me to join them. Their faces radiated with exuberance, the joy that only the young can project.

At that moment, I had no recollection of where I had been. I only knew that this was life at its absolute apex. I was here, and it was real, and I never wanted to leave.

Then things grew dark, and I was thinking that I didn't want to leave. *I must be having a nightmare.* I felt my bare chest with my fingertips. The medics had stripped me of my clothing.

Oh, yeah, I was on the way to the hospital, with a heart attack or something. But, that was just a bad dream. I should be with those young people. I'll soon come out of this dream, or whatever it is…

But I was on the stretcher, and a man was saying, "I had to hit him with the paddles."

"What paddles?" I remember asking.

"Your heart stopped, and I had to use the paddles," he said.

They said I came back chattering—asking questions and telling things.

I sure did! I had just been in the most wonderful place, and I wanted to tell them about it. Most of all, I wanted to see it again.

Dreams, even the most vivid ones, are most often nonsensical. They usually fade and are soon forgotten. But the young people and the brilliant ambience of that place hasn't faded to the moment of this writing.

One significant remembrance is that I was *instantaneously* in that heavenly presence when my heart stopped. When one passes out or is anesthetized, the mind goes completely black. One awakes, then, when the consciousness returns and there is no memory of any sort of dream. But during what I experienced that day as the pain in my chest became excruciating, there was no black-out—no fading in or out as in the dream state. The sense of reality is what stays in my mind's eye. The impact of that experience grows rather than diminishes.

MY SECOND LAST HEARTBEAT

Someone was working in the area of the groin on my right side. I remember thinking something about the fact the medics were probably doing an angiogram, a procedure I had heard about from friends who had been given them.

Still, I asked, "What are you doing?"

The man bent over me said in accented English: "No details."

Another man, off to my left, said, "He's busy trying to save your life."

I thought, *Best to just keep the mouth shut when someone is trying to save your life.* So I did.

Somewhere during all of this, I felt the pain grow to an intolerable level in my chest. I then heard the electronic-sounding noise again.

TERRY JAMES—I was again facing those wonder-ful, beautiful young people. They were even more joyous in beckoning me to join them—in expressing their great exultation—than the first time. The peace I sensed, in spite of the dynamic ebullience, was awe-inspiring.

I was riveted by the luminescent, smiling face of one particular young woman in the throng. She had been the main object of my attention in the first time I had faced them, too, I now remember. I was about to move into their midst.

But, it wasn't to be. My surroundings again grew dark, and I had the same realization I had experienced earlier: I was leaving the place I wanted to be forever. The nightmare had returned, the reality of life that truly matters left behind.

My Third Last Heartbeat

I'm amazed as I reflect on these life-or-death episodes. Not once did I have any anxiety whatsoever that I might die. It just never crossed my mind. My thoughts were focused on that place I had been twice. I didn't even realize that I *saw* during those times with perfect vision, despite the fact I'm totally blind. These real-izations would all come later.

My sense was that all was well under control. Margaret said later that the doctors told her they would do all they could for me, but it was said in tones that indicated they expected the worst. I had, they told her, been dead on arrival.

But, back to the ongoing drama at that moment in the emergency room when I heard the *blip* again.

TERRY JAMES—This time, I was among the young people, and felt the radiance of their love for me encompass—permeate—me. I was a visceral part of this group of heavenly young people!

We were moving swiftly from left to right, whether running or being moved along in some other manner, I don't know. The same laughing young woman had her beautiful face turned toward me. Her arms and hands, like those of all within our group, were thrust upward in a gesture of celebration. We were headed in the direction of some spectacular magnetism that drew us with a force we neither could nor wanted to resist.

But, I wouldn't find out where.

Everything dissolved to black, and I was again on the table in the cardiac care unit.

I found out later from my interventional cardiologist, Dr. Rao, that I had suffered what they call a widow maker—named so for obvious reasons. "Fifty percent of those with this don't live to get to the ER," he said. "Of those who do get to the ER, not many live." In his estimation, I was within ten seconds of my heart not being able to be restarted with the paddles.

Talk about a brush with death! Ten more seconds and I wouldn't have been able to come back and describe anything to anyone. But obviously I did come back, and because I believe God has a purpose for everything (see Jeremiah 29:11 and Romans 8:28, for example), I've been trying to make sense out of what I saw, heard, and felt, and to research how it fits within what the Bible says about Heaven.

Here's one of my first—and deepest—impressions: I wasn't in a dark tunnel, fading into unconsciousness, or drifting off to sleep. In fact, I've never been more awake in my life.

"THE FINAL AWAKENING"

"The Grave the last sleep?—no; it is the final awakening."

Sir Walter Scott[3]

"Think of yourself just as a seed patiently waiting in the earth: waiting to come up a flower in the Gardener's good time, up into the real world, the real waking. I suppose that our whole present life, looked back on from there, will seem only a drowsy half-waking. We are here in the land of dreams. But cock-crow is coming."

C. S. Lewis[4]

Throughout the ages, in literature and art, "sleep" has been a common way to describe death. A distraught Hamlet, after learning that his uncle has killed his father and married his mother, considers suicide, saying: "To die, to sleep-/No more."[5] The title of a late eighteenth-century painting entitled "The Last Sleep of Arthur in Avalon" by Edward Burne-Jones relies on the same metaphor to express the death of the beloved king. The lyrics to several songs in the theater production of Les Miserables refer to death as "sleep": "I will stay with you/Till you are sleeping," a young revolutionary pledges to his faithful friend as she lays dying from a fatal wound. And at the end of a long and turbulent life, author Victor Hugo's lead character, Jean Valjean, asks his daughter to hear his words of confession after he has passed on, "when I at last am sleeping."

"Sleep" is an especially often-used euphemism for death throughout the pages of Scripture. The apostle Paul, in 1 Corinthians 11:30, said that "many sleep" to explain that numerous people had died as a consequence of failing to examine themselves before taking the Lord's Supper. He used the same word

in his brief eulogy of David in Acts 13:36: "For David, after he had
served the purpose of God in his own generation, *fell asleep,* and
was laid among his fathers and underwent decay" (emphasis
added).[6]

It's important to realize, however, that the use of the word
"sleeping" to refer to death in Scripture points only to physical
death, not to any kind of eternal existence. A lifeless body, after
all, does look like it's asleep, and appears—actually, *is*—"devoid
of any sensation or awareness," as John MacArthur points out in
his book, *The Glory of Heaven.*[7]

WHAT HAPPENS RIGHT AFTER DEATH

As I've stated already, and as I will probably say again in order to
make sure I'm perfectly clear: I was only on the *brink* of death. My
experience, needless to say, made me very curious: What would
have happened had my heart not resumed its beating? I believe
we find the answer in Scripture, which describes at least three
things that happen to Christ-followers during the moments just
after death.

1. **When we die, our souls reach their after-life desti-
    nation *immediately.*** "When I was killed, I was instantly
    transported to heaven's gate," says Don Piper, author of
    90 Minutes in Heaven, who was pronounced dead at the

scene when the vehicle he was driving home from a minister's conference collided with an eighteen-wheeler. "It was an instantaneous thing."[8] Contrary to all the clichés and jokes about Heaven making the circuit, there's no line to stand in at the Pearly Gate, no waiting room to sit in before gaining entry, and no check-in area where St. Peter stands to take down names and check reservations like a host in the lobby of a busy restaurant.

The journey is instant.

"Everything in Scripture indicates that the believer's entrance to heaven occurs immediately upon death," MacArthur states.[9] When Christian martyr Stephen was moments away from death by stoning, he prayed, "Lord Jesus, receive my spirit!" (Acts 7:59), indicating the imminence of the moment his spirit would join Christ's presence. The Lord Himself succinctly conveyed this idea when He told the believing thief on the cross beside Him: "*Today* you shall be with Me in Paradise" (Luke 23:43, emphasis added). And Paul, in saying that he prefers to be "absent from the body and to be at home with the Lord" (2 Corinthians 5:8), expressed the truth that once the soul leaves the body, it is ushered to its after-life destination pronto. Right away. I had a distinct sense of the speed of that occurrence when, in the split-second that I heard the computer-like noise, I was no longer in my earthly surroundings.

2. **The after-life destination, for believers, is initially an "intermediate" state.** Make no mistake: This "intermediate" state (or "present Heaven," as Bible scholar Randy Alcorn calls it) is Heaven, all right, with all of its promised goodness and perfection, but it is not our final destination for all of eternity. (Nor is it purgatory, which, as taught in the Roman Catholic tradition, is a place where those who have died undergo a time of cleansing in order to become holy enough to enter Heaven. Jesus purchased our purity on the cross with His own blood, in fact, *becoming* our sin, as Paul phrased it in 2 Corinthians 5:21, and that purification isn't still in progress; "it is finished"—as proclaimed by the crucified Christ in John 19:30.) Rather, this intermediate state is a "transitional period between our past lives on Earth and our future resurrection to life on the New Earth."[10, 11]

3. **After death, our souls remain fully conscious.**

Partly because Scripture does, as mentioned earlier, often refer to death as sleep, some throughout history have held to the doctrine of soul sleep, which teaches that upon death we go into a state of unconsciousness where we remain until Christ returns and raises us to eternal life. This is simply not scriptural, however, for many reasons. The passages we've already mentioned, Luke 23:43 and 2 Corinthians 5:8, indicate that an alertness will be experienced by those who pass from life on Earth to eternal life in Heaven. Biblical scholar Wayne Grudem points out that the awareness isn't limited to some type of self-awareness and an understanding of what is going on around us in Heaven; it extends to the point that we will know what's going on even on Earth:

The fact that Hebrews 12:1 says, "We are surrounded by so great a cloud of witnesses," just after an entire chapter spent on the discussion of the faith of Old Testament saints who had died (Hebrews 11), and the fact that the author encourages us to run the race of life with perseverance because we are surrounded by this great cloud of witnesses, both suggest that those who have died and gone before have some awareness of what is going on in the earth.[12]

Interestingly, "awake" and its synonyms are by far the more common words than those having to do with being "asleep" in accounts of those who have had near-death experiences. Consider the words of Boris Pilipshuk describing the moment when he believes his spirit left his body while doctors were scrambling to save his life after he had been rushed to the hospital following a brain hemorrhage:

BORIS PILIPSHUK—It felt as if I was conscious. I began seeing with my own eyes.... I began seeing everything as if from above. My spirit came out of me and looked at my body.[13]

Dr. Gerard Landry, whose near-death experience during a heart attack is recorded in Rita Bennett's book, *To Heaven and Back*, says:

> **GERARD LANDRY**—I knew I was in another world— a world that is as real as this world is to anyone reading this. What I saw, I saw with the eyes of the spirit, because at that time my soul and my spirit were in heaven. At the time you leave the flesh, your spiritual awareness becomes acute, because the flesh holds down your spiritual awareness. At death, your spirit is released. My experience was supernatural but nonetheless real.[14]

Awake! As I said earlier, I, like Mr. Pilipshuk and Dr. Landry, can't think of a more accurate word to describe my state of being when my heart stopped. My senses were heightened and I noticed even the smallest details of my surroundings.

"The spiritual part of us relocates to a conscious existence in Heaven (Daniel 12:2–3; 2 Corinthians 5:8)," notes Randy Alcorn. "Every reference in Revelation to human beings talking and worshiping in Heaven prior to the resurrection of the dead demonstrates that our spiritual beings are conscious, not sleeping, after death."[15] The story Jesus told of the rich man and Lazarus (see Luke 16:19–31) is one of the best biblical illustrations of the truth that the souls of those who have died are fully aware of the goings-on around them. Not only were Lazarus and the rich man conscious in Heaven and Hell immediately after they died, but the concrete details furnished in that account suggest a keen sensory awareness.

Being aware of what's going on around us in Heaven—rather than in some kind of a sleepy fog—just might be one of its sweetest blessings. After all, who would want to miss even one detail of the dwelling place of Love Himself?

Chapter Two

LOVED!

"For I am convinced that neither death, nor life, nor angels, nor principalities, nor things present, nor things to come, nor powers, nor height, nor depth, nor any other created thing, will be able to separate us from the love of God, which is in Christ Jesus our Lord" (Romans 8:38–39).

TERRY JAMES—Love was the first magnificent expression of that heavenly realm I sensed. It was a warmth that penetrated my innermost thoughts.

DARREL YOUNG—I dreaded going back into that body of mine, but I dreaded more leaving that love, joy and peace that I had experienced with Jesus…. It is now my desire to tell as many people as I can about the love of Jesus for them…. When He held my hand for six hours and thirty-five minutes earth time, He showed me what total love and total peace is, and I will never be the same again.[16]

A recurring theme among those who have had a near-death experience is the overwhelming sense of love they feel. One major difference sets my experience apart from that of Darrel Young, whose brush with death occurred when he went into cardiac arrest in the operating room before a scheduled heart surgery. The love I felt sprang from the fellowship I was having with the cheering group of people, whereas the love he described accompanied his encounter with Jesus. Both "loves" were all encompassing, and the Bible tells us that both expressions of love are exactly what believers can expect to enjoy in Heaven. Scripture promises that we will experience love—a profound, perfected love unhindered by fleshly limitations—with friends and relatives, with all of those who have gone on to Heaven before us, with the angelic citizens of Heaven, and with our Heavenly Father Himself.

A FAMILY'S LOVE

RICHARD WRIGHT—I opened one eye and looked over to the door of the Emergency Room, and there stood my grandma, my grandpa, my aunt, and my cousin, all of whom had died years ago, just standing at the doorway smiling and waving for me to come on! I was amazed to see them, and quickly found myself through the door and out into the hallway. My mother-in-law, who had died about eleven years previously, came up to me and hugged me.[17]

> **DON PIPER**—I did not see a single person that I did not know. They were relatives, they were friends that died in high school, they were teachers—they were people I had seen and known all my life who had gone to glory. They were smiling; they were embracing me; they were welcoming me. They were in the process of taking me through the gate of heaven.[18]

A great longing of the human heart—and often the only hope that helps us navigate the pain of a loved one's death—is that we might be able to see friends and relatives who passed away before us again one day in Heaven. The Bible makes it clear that this isn't just wishful thinking. In 1 Thessalonians 4, it's a truth Paul relies on to encourage believers and remind them that they can have joy and hope rather than grief and despair when thinking about those who have preceded them in death.

"What a comfort we as believers have in the promise that someday we will be reunited with those whom we love in Christ," Dr. W. A. Criswell states in the book, *Heaven*. "This hope is incomparably sweet and dear beyond words to describe it."[19]

The Lord created us for fellowship not just with Him but with other people: "It is not good for the man to be alone," the Creator God states (see Genesis 2:18). And "two are better than one," the wise Solomon observes as he ponders the meaning of life (Ecclesiastes 4:9). With this in mind, it stands to reason that the loving relationships that begin on Earth among those who are members of the family of God would withstand physical death and endure into eternity.

What is the biblical basis of this truth, which theologians call the "doctrine of heavenly recognition"? There is much evidence in God's Word.

A Gathering beyond the Grave

In the Old Testament, the phrase "gathered unto his people" is often used to describe an individual's death (see Genesis 25:8; 35:29; and 49:33). While this phrase might be one way of describing the act of burying someone in the family plot, thus allowing the person to be physically returned to relatives who preceded him or her in death, in a sense, the context of these passages indicates a much larger meaning. Consider that after Abraham died, Scripture states that he was "gathered to his people"—but he was buried in a cave in Mamre in Canaan, hundreds of miles away from where his ancestors would have been laid to rest. This tells us that the phrase "gathered unto his people" indicates a family reunion *beyond* the graveyard— a celebratory regathering in the afterlife, with the ability to recognize one's "people" implicit in that event.

The Basis of Great Comfort

David—the man after God's own heart who became Israel's greatest king—finds comfort after the death of his infant son in thoughts of being able to join the child after death: "Can I bring him back again?" the distraught father cries in 2 Samuel 12:23. "I will go to him, but he will not return to me." That David will know who his son is when he "goes to him" after death is an understood premise of David's expression. By extension, we can believe that we will see our loved ones with a full awareness of who they are.

Closer than Ever

As exciting as the idea of recognizing and reuniting with our loved ones in Heaven is the fact that we will know them in a way that's far more meaningful than we do on Earth. "In fact, we won't really know each other *until* we get to heaven," says Mark Hitchcock. "Only in heaven, when all the masks and facades are torn away, will we really know one another and enjoy intimate, unhindered fellowship."[20]

Think about it: Every aspect of our earthly relationships is colored to one degree or another by our human nature, which is innately unwise, almost uncontrollably selfish, and yes, inherently sinful. For example, you may love a certain friend, but his betrayal of a confidence years ago has stifled your ability to trust him. Or you may enjoy a close relationship with another person, but you are too insecure—perhaps even too proud—to completely let down your guard with her and share your biggest dreams and most worrisome concerns. Like a film of sea spray on the camera lens obstructs the clarity and beauty of a snapshot of the sunrise over the surf, these all-too-human hang-ups and misgivings blur and distort the quality of our relationships in the here and now. When in Heaven the spirit is no longer held captive by our humanity, broken and damaged by the promised trials and troubles of this world, we will enjoy fellowship on a whole new level—giving and receiving the love mentioned in John 15:12 in a way we've never been able to do before: "Love one another *as I have loved you*" (emphasis added).

Never Meet a Stranger

Further, and just as thrilling, is that not only will we recognize the people with whom we had relationships in our earthly lives, but we will also recognize those we didn't personally know. Check the passages in Matthew 17:1–9, Mark 9:2–8, and Luke 9:28–36 describing the Transfiguration, that moment high upon the mountaintop when Jesus was changed from His human form into His glorified state. When Moses and Elijah appeared on the scene, talking with Jesus, the disciples clearly knew who they were—even though the patriarch and the prophet had lived and died many centuries before the disciples were born. This scene "is generally accepted as strong evidence of Heavenly Recognition," says Bible scholar and preacher Lehman Strauss. "After death the spirit is clothed with a spirit body that is recognizable.... Not only were Moses and Elijah recognizable by our Lord, but they were known to the disciples also."[21]

Do you realize what that means? Even though you've never met them, the "heroes of the Scriptures will be your neighbors in heaven!"[22] Apparently, we'll get to spend eternity getting to know one another better as we all join together, perfectly united in love. Our common focus will be fixed on a singular, breathtaking task: worshipping the Lord. In his blog, Randy Alcorn states:

> Some falsely assume that when we give attention to people it automatically distracts us from God. But even now, in a fallen world, people can turn my attention to God. Was Jesus distracted from God by spending time with people on Earth? Certainly not. In Heaven, no person will distract us from God. We will never experience any conflict between worshiping God himself and enjoying God's people. Our source of comfort isn't only that we'll be with the Lord in Heaven but also that we'll be with each other. We'll sit at feasts not only with God, but with his people. That is his design, and we should look forward to it.[23]

Will We See Our Pets?
We can hardly talk about reunions with loved ones in Heaven without raising one of the most frequently asked ques-

tions about the life that follows physical death: Do our pets go to Heaven when they die? Having loved more four-legged friends than I can count in my lifetime, I did some research on the topic several years ago. While there is some disagreement about this among biblical scholars, and in fact we won't know for sure until we get there, what I learned was enough to convince me that, yes, animals will be in Heaven.

We know from Scripture that animals, like people, are beings that have spirits (see Exodus 3:21). Further, creatures ranging from wolves and lions to cattle and snakes appear in passages describing the millennial kingdom, the thousand-year reign of Christ, indicating that they will indeed exist in eternity (see Isaiah 11:6–8).

"Animals were part of the original creation of God that was declared 'good,'" states Mark Hitchcock. "The Garden of Eden, called Paradise, was filled with animals (Genesis 1:25). Revelation tells us that Heaven will contain many of the same things that were in the original creation, such as a river, trees, and fruit. Why not animals too?"[24]

We'll Be Hanging Out with the Angels!
We know from Scripture that angels—multitudes of them!—are carrying on the business of Heaven on Earth—perhaps even right under our noses.

"Holy angels have been active in the affairs of God and man since their creation," says author and speaker Bob Glaze. "They live to serve and are spectators observing the events of mankind.... They stand by awaiting the Lord to command them to intervene in the lives of the saints, for they are ministering spirits—perhaps every one assigned to a different person."[25]

While we don't see angels on Earth, except perhaps in very rare instances,[26] Scripture indicates that our death marks the beginning of a whole new relationship with these magnificent and mysterious beings.

"One of the best parts of heaven may be getting to know and fellowshipping with angels," Joni Eareckson Tada says in her book, *Heaven...Your Real Home*. "They love God and they enjoy us."[27]

Possibly the first and most loving kindness the Lord shows us upon our physical death—and one widely reported by those who have had glimpses into glory—is the gift of an angelic shepherd or shepherds to guide us from this world into eternity (see Luke 16:22, Luke 24:51; Acts 1:9; Jude 1:9). Royston Fraser, a missionary, recalls that shortly after being shot in the stomach while working with a Christian organization in a politically troubled area of Chile, he was well aware of this heavenly escort:

> **ROYSTON FRASER**—I became aware of where I was when, quite suddenly, I found myself standing in the air—suspended, as it were, in space—looking at my body on the operating table. After a few moments two angels came along and said, "This way."

We travelled along a dark passage, but all the time I could see a light at the end. When we got to the end of the tunnel it was like going through thick cobwebs, and into the most marvelous place I had ever dreamed of.[28]

Gerard Sybers, who flatlined after going into anaphylactic shock during an allergic reaction to medication, remembers not only being with angels, but having the distinct sense of being carried by them:

GERARD SYBERS—I found myself in the presence of three heavenly beings, in long flowing white robes, who were carrying me carefully upon their hands. I could however not make out their faces, as they gently carried me away. Then I realized that I must have died, so I asked them where they were taking me. Now the language was an unspoken one, language proceeded by thought. They informed me that they were instructed to take me to the City of the great King.[29]

And Betty Malz, pronounced dead in July 1959 in Terre Haute, Indiana, when she was twenty-seven years old, shares in her book, *My Glimpse of Eternity*, that she had no fear in death—perhaps because of the fact that she realized she wasn't alone.

BETTY MALZ—Then I realized I was not walking alone. To the left, and a little behind me, strode a tall, masculine-looking figure in a robe. I wondered if he were an angel and tried to see if he had wings. But he was facing me and I could not see his back. I sensed, however, that he could go anywhere he wanted and very quickly.

We did not speak to each other. Somehow it didn't seem necessary, for we were both going in the same direction. Then I became aware that he was not a stranger. He knew me and I felt a strange kinship with him. Where had we met? Had we always known each other? It seemed we had.[30]

These accounts, although varied in detail, point to the truth that "the Bible guarantees every believer an escorted journey into the presence of Christ by the holy angels," notes Billy Graham.[31] He, Dr. David Jeremiah, and others suggest that this heavenly assistance has to do with ensuring the safe crossing of our souls across the final stretch of "enemy territory" in this world, where Satan rules and likely has demons positioned to wage one last-ditch effort to win our souls.[32]

Once we're safely ushered to our destination and begin hobnobbing around Heaven with the angels, we can expect to see them carrying out a busy and productive existence in this other dimension. They are distinctly organized, with ranks and responsibilities, and their activities include celebrating the salvation of repentant sinners (Luke 15:10) and worshipping

around the throne of God. We will join these magnificent beings in many of these activities.[33] (We will discuss more about
what we'll be doing in Heaven in chapter 6.)

———•———

It gives me great comfort and pleasure to think about experiencing the love of Heaven by interacting with the angels—
some of whom have no doubt been making it their business
to keep me from harm all the days of my life. I also look forward
with excitement to enjoying the rekindled love of friends and
family members who have been separated from me by death.
I wonder with excitement which of the biblical saints—especially those on my own roster of heroes in the faith—I'll get to
shake hands with first. And I'll be very honest: "Reunion with
Buckley," my bulldog who died, is way up there on my list of
the many things I look forward to when I reach Heaven.

But, of course, none of these is an all-consuming focus of my
thoughts about life after life. At the very top of that list of
things I'm anticipating in Heaven is meeting my Lord—Love
Himself—face to face.

THE FATHER'S FELLOWSHIP

"We will see Him just as He is" (1 John 3:2).

"As for me, I shall behold Your face in righteousness; I will be satisfied with Your likeness when I awake" (Psalm 17:15).

"And I heard a loud voice from the throne, saying, 'Behold, the tabernacle of God is among men, and He will dwell among them, and they shall be His people, and God Himself will be among them'" (Revelation 21:3).

"Being with God is the heart and soul of Heaven. Every other heavenly pleasure will derive from and be secondary to his presence. God's greatest gift to us is, and always will be, himself."

Randy Alcorn[34]

Perhaps the most striking fact about my near-death experience is that I did not enter the presence of Jesus. Scripture makes it clear that we will see Jesus after death; for support of this, we only need to revisit verses we've looked at already.

"Today you shall be with Me in Paradise," Jesus told the thief on the cross, assuring him that the relationship between the two had only just begun (Luke 23:43). Before the day was over, they would *be together,* in very different surroundings and circumstances.

And, again, Paul emphasized that absence from the body means presence with the Lord (2 Corinthians 5:8)—further pointing out that departing this life to be with Christ "is very much better" (Philippians 1:23) than remaining a part of the living population on Earth. As Ron Rhodes puts it, "Our Lord is with us during life, and He will meet us face-to-face at the moment of death" (Philippians 1:21–23; 2 Corinthians 5:8)."[35]

As wonderful as I found the moments in which I was in that space between life and death, I can't even begin to fathom the wonder of what it will be like to enter the Lord's presence in Heaven.

Being with God. Seeing Jesus. Who can come up with words adequate to express how amazing that will be? No wonder those whose glimpses into glory have given them personal encounters with the Lord say their lives will never be the same:

> **GEORGE RITCHIE**—I thought suddenly, "This is death. This is what we human beings call 'death,' this splitting from one's self." It was the first time I had connected death with what had happened to me.
>
> In that most despairing moment, the little room began to fill with light. I say "light," but there is no word in our language to describe brilliance that intense.

I must try to find words, however, because incomprehensible as the experience was to my intellect, it has affected every moment of my life since then. The light that entered that room was Christ: I knew because a thought was put deep within me: "You are in the presence of the Son of God." I could have called Him "light," but I could also have said "love," for that room was flooded, pierced, illuminated, by the most total compassion I have ever felt. It was a presence so comforting, so joyous and all satisfying, that I wanted to lose myself forever in the wonder of it.[36]

GERARD SYBERS—I did not go through any tunnel, nor saw any family members, but was instantly transported to a city of light, and was brought before the Great King, whom, I might add, treated me like a son coming home from battle. He showed intense emotions, and let me know that He was in love with me and all those who profess His Name. It was his desire to keep me there, but the decision to go back was mine, and I realized that I had much work to do for His Name's sake.[37]

DARREL YOUNG—The robe that He was wearing was very beautiful, far more beautiful than I can describe. There was a very bright light coming from Him. It was so bright that it could never have been produced by a thousand powerful lights. It was not like the sunlight on Earth that would cause you to squint your eyes. I had always thought of His robe

> as being white, like the whitest cloth that one could imagine. But what I saw was clear, pure white gold that flowed like cloth, as it says in Matthew 17:2: "His face shone like the sun, and his clothes became as white as the light."[38]

Intimate, personal fellowship with the Father is the most staggering promise of Heaven and the grand finale (although there is nothing really "final" about eternity) to the true-life story of a God who has desired nothing more than to lavish His love on and enjoy fellowship with people since before He even created them.

In a word, the theme of that story is love, and because "the love of an eternal God must be an eternal love,"[39] we know that it:

- **Commenced** in eternity past: "And in Your book were all written the days that were ordained for me, when as yet there was not one of them" (Psalm 139:16).

- **Continues** into eternity present: "Where two or three have gathered together in My name, I am there in their midst" (Matthew 28:20; see also Psalm 14:5).

- **Culminates** in eternity future: "I have loved you with an everlasting love; therefore I have drawn you with lovingkindness" (Jeremiah 31:3).

In the world today, the existence of love is the most compelling evidence of the existence of God, for "God is love" (1 John 4:16). His love for us is perfect and so vast that He sent His own Son to die on the cross for our sins, assuring anyone who accepts that gift a place with Him in Heaven: "But God, being rich in mercy, because of His great love with which He loved us, even when we were dead in our transgressions, made us alive together with Christ" (Ephesians 2:4–5).

Amazingly, our presence in Heaven begins the moment we take that step. We're told that at the moment we entrust our lives to the Lord, He "raise[s] us up with Him, and seat[s] us with Him in the heavenly places in Christ Jesus" (Ephesians 2:6).

It's a mind-boggling concept: We're already seated in Heaven with Christ? How is that possible, while we're logging onto computers at very earthly jobs, driving our cars along very Earth-bound highways, and participating in other very mortal activities?

Harold W. Hoehner, professor of New Testament studies at Dallas Theological Seminary, explains it this way:

> Believers are positioned spiritually in heaven, where Christ is. They are no longer mere earthlings; their citizenship is in heaven (Philippians 3:20). He is the exalted Son of God, and they are exalted sons and

daughters of God. These actions of God toward unbelievers are similar to what God did for Christ: "He
raised Him from the dead and seated Him at His
right hand in the heavenly realms" (Ephesians 1:20).
Whereas Christ had died physically (1:20), unbelievers were dead spiritually (2:1–3). While Christ was
raised physically (1:20), unbelievers are made alive
and raised with Christ spiritually (2:5–6). Christ is
seated in the heavenly realms physically...but believers are seated with Christ in the heavenly realms
spiritually (2:6).[40]

So, even though we are spiritually seated in Heaven, our physical feet are firmly planted on the turf of this planet. And while
we're here, because of the limitations imposed on us by our
sinful nature, we can neither see the Lord (Exodus 33:20) nor
enjoy His love in its fullest expression (1 Corinthians 13:9, 12).

But all that will change once our spirits are freed by death. We
will see Him "just as He is" (1 John 3:2), and for the first time
ever, we will fully "be able to comprehend with all the saints...
the breadth and length and height and depth" of Christ's love
(Ephesians 3:18–19).

Understanding the incomprehensible—it's a staggering
thought. "In the afterlife there will no longer be intermittent
fellowship with the Lord, blighted by sin and defeat," says Ron
Rhodes. "Instead, it will be continuous.... To fellowship with
God is the essence of heavenly life, the fount and source of
all blessing. We may be confident that the crowning wonder

of our experience in the eternal city will be the perpetual and endless exploration of that unutterable beauty, majesty, love, holiness, power, joy, and grace which is God Himself."[41]

In Heaven, we will finally see the face no human can look at and live. "For many of us, the very sight of His face will be heaven enough," says author Beth Moore. "We are not unlike Moses who experienced God's presence but could not see His face. To him and to all confined momentarily by mortality, God has said, 'You cannot see my face, for no one may see me and live' (Exodus 33:10). When all is said and done, we who are alive in Christ will indeed see his face and live. Happily ever after." [42]

Chapter Three

RESTORED!

*"Then the eyes of the blind will be opened
And the ears of the deaf will be unstopped" (Isaiah 35:5).*

TERRY JAMES—I had no fuzziness about any part of what I saw, but didn't think about seeing or not seeing. I had no notion: I am really blind, so why am I seeing? As a matter of fact, I had no thought whatsoever of anything earthly. I could make out vivid detail, although it was all so brief. I remember that the clothing was unlike any I've ever seen. All different colors—very brilliant in color—as I recall, almost uniform-like, yet no two of the young people had the same outfit. Brilliant light, in many colors, seemed to constitute the ambient surroundings.

The intricate details of this glimpse into Heaven come from a man who, as I sit here writing at my computer, sees only a totally opaque whiteness—or really, more of a very light gray. I can make out no details whatsoever because, as readers are well aware by now, I'm blind.

The depression was overwhelming after I returned home from that visit to the retinal specialist in Little Rock, Arkansas, in the spring of 1977. The doctor had just confirmed the diagnosis of the ophthalmologist who had referred me. I had *retinitis pigmentosa,* and it would almost without question lead to total blindness.

I had a wife, a six-year old son, and a career in advertising and public relations, in which I relied heavily on my background in and passion for visual arts. The news was devastating, and I went into a depressive tailspin. For three full days and nights, I wallowed in self-pity and all of the emotions of what the prospects for blindness might mean. I wasn't even thirty-five years old yet! I asked—no, *begged*—the Lord to take the disease from me...to heal my eyes.

But there was no answer, and the depression grew worse.

Finally, I remembered the words spoken by the apostle Paul, who had asked the Lord to remove a particular ailment—a "thorn" that, I believe, was related to his vision. "I implored the Lord three times that it might leave me," Paul had said. And the Lord answered, "My grace is sufficient for you, for power is perfected in weakness" (2 Corinthians 12:8–9).

The Lord's response to Paul's plea compelled me to realize that I should be making a different request to the Lord. Rather than asking, "Please remove my blindness," I asked, "Please, Lord, if you won't take the disease from me, please take all of the fear about it out of my mind."

As He is my witness, all my fear about going blind was instantly gone, and I haven't had any apprehension about losing my eyesight since. Maybe His grace allowing me to keep my focus off of my blindness and, instead, always upon Him is why the thought *I can see!* wasn't my first memory of what happened after my heart stopped beating. It was only well after the fact, after I was out of danger and recovering, that I mentally processed the truth that, yes, I had been able to see during my glimpse into glory—and with better than 20/20 vision.

A NEW BODY

"The Lord Jesus Christ…will transform the body of our humble state into conformity with the body of His glory" (Philippians 3:20–21).

Somewhere in my broken, paralyzed body is the seed of what I shall become. The paralysis makes what I am to become all the more grand when you contrast atrophied, useless legs against splendorous resurrected legs. I'm convinced that if there are mirrors in heaven (and why not?), the image I'll see will be unmistakably "Joni," although a much better, brighter Joni.

Joni Eareckson Tada[43]

That during my heavenly experience I could see with eyes that had been blind for so many years shouldn't surprise, because restoration of infirmities is yet another breathtaking promise the Bible offers about Heaven. Our current, "humble" bodies, as the verse above describes them, will become like Christ's glorified body was after His resurrection—meaning that they will be perfect in every way.

And who doesn't want—many of us desperately—to look forward to healing and restoration in one way or another? Even when we don't have pressing physiological issues such as blindness, deafness, heart trouble, diabetes, or cancer, our health is still on the decline as we live out our years. Each decade we track through brings new reminders of our bodies' finite qualities. The taut flesh of youth begins to sag and wrinkle; the strength—whether used to carry a child or open a jar—wanes; the ability to recall facts from earlier today or twelve years ago declines. All this is because our bodies are subject to the effects of living in a fallen, imperfect world. The Bible describes our current bodies with words such as "lowly," "perishable," "humble," and "weak." However, terms used to describe our after-death bodies in Heaven indicate that they will be quite the opposite: "glorious," "imperishable," and "powerful." These bodies must undergo a great makeover in order for them to be properly outfitted for life in God's perfect, eternal kingdom!

That kind of dramatic transformation—from lowly to glorious, perishable to imperishable, and weak to powerful—doesn't call for mere healing or reconstruction; it requires an "ultimate extreme makeover," as author Mark Hitchcock calls the overhaul every believer in Jesus Christ will get someday. Far from cosmetic fixes and temporary tweaks, it will be an all-out replacement, as indicated in the promise Jesus Christ offers to the Heaven-bound: "Behold, I am making all things new" (Revelation 21:5).

Not all of the details of what that newness entails are included in the Bible, but we can find plenty of information to give us at least a hint of what's to come. Hitchcock presents a thought-provoking list of what we can learn from Scripture about our new bodies in his book, *55 Answers to Questions about Life After Death:*

1. They will never be subject to disease, decay, or death. They will be imperishable.

2. They will be perfectly suitable to our new environment. They will be "heavenly" bodies.

3. They will each be unique and diverse from one another. Just as different stars and planets are unique and have varying degrees of glory, we will each maintain a uniqueness and diversity in heaven.

4. They will be vastly superior to our present bodies.

5. They will be glorious—"full of glory." They will never disappoint us.

6. They will be powerful. The future body will be an invincible fortress.

7. They will be spiritual, not natural. This doesn't mean they won't be real or physical. It simply means that our new body will allow us to fully express our spiritual nature. Unlike our present natural body, our future body will be unaffected by the physical laws of gravity and space.

8. They will have continuity with our present body, yet be vastly changed.[44]

"Do I know what we'll look like in heaven?" Billy Graham asks. "No—but our new bodies will be perfect, beyond the reach of all illness and decay."[45] This brings to mind my own experience, when the group of people I saw so vividly beckoned me to join them during the moments I was experiencing physical death during my heart attack. The people I saw were noticeably youthful and healthy—that is one of the details that stands out the most from my memory. Not coincidentally, healthfulness and youth are conditions very much in keeping with what theologians say about our resurrected bodies will be like:

> The fact that our new bodies will be "imperishable" means that they will not wear out or grow old or ever be subject to any kind of sickness or disease. They will be completely healthy and strong forever. Moreover, since the gradual process of aging is part of the process by which our bodies now are subject to "corruption," it is appropriate to think that our resurrection bodies will have no sign of aging, but will have the

characteristics of youthful but mature manhood or womanhood forever.[46]

Perhaps it is a sampling of this kind of perfection and renewal that Dr. Richard Eby had during his near-death experience, which he describes in his book, *A Physician's Amazing Account of Being "Caught Up Into Paradise."* He reports having a keen awareness that not only were his ailments removed, but he was in a new body altogether:

> RICHARD EBY—I was enjoying a heavenly "body"; I was totally me. Aside from the complete absence of pain and the total presence of peace (neither of which I had ever known on earth), I looked like me, felt like me, reacted like me. I was me. I simply suddenly had shed the old body and was now living anew in this fantastic cloud-like body![47]

And although Dr. Eby didn't have visual troubles like mine, he reports that his sight was greatly improved: "Instantly," he says, "my eyes were unlimited in range of vision. Ten inches or ten miles—the focus was sharp and clear."

In her book, *My Glimpse of Eternity,* Betty Malz also describes a distinct sensation of renewal during the moments when she found herself on the other side of a transition to a place outside time and experience as she knew them.

BETTY MALZ—Despite three incisions in my body from the operations, I stood erect without pain.... There was no darkness, no uncertainty, only a change in location and a total sense of well being.[48]

On Earth, we catch colds, develop heart conditions, and endure chronic illnesses. These kinds of ailments cause us no end of frustration, pain, and suffering. But in Heaven, that won't be true. There will "no longer be any curse" (Revelation 22:3), therefore there will no longer be any suffering—whether physically, mentally, or emotionally. "He will wipe away every tear from their eyes," is the promise we're given. "There will no longer be any death; there will no longer be any mourning, or crying, or pain; the first things have passed away" (Revelation 21:4).

Distress of any kind will be absent; in its place we'll only experience wholeness and joy. "Heaven will be a world where 'the eyes of the blind will be opened and the ears of the deaf unstopped. And the lame will leap like a deer, and the mute tongue will shout for joy' (Isaiah 35:5–6)," explains one writer. "There will be no more suffering in heaven."[49]

When Will We Receive these New Bodies?
The subject of Heaven raises many mind-bending theological questions, and talk of the present Heaven—the Heaven we enter immediately upon death and the one we remain in until the Rapture—seems to complicate the issues even further.

Paul's words in 1 Thessalonians 4:16 shed some light. He states that at the time of the Rapture, when the Lord "descend[s] from heaven with a shout, with the voice of the archangel and with the trumpet of God," those who have died as believers "rise first." In other words, this time will not only be marked by a reunion in the clouds above the earth among members of the family of God, but it will also be marked by the reuniting of dead believers with their earthly bodies. When Jesus descends from Heaven to gather together His family of believers, those who have already died—whose spirits are already in Heaven with the Lord—will be united with their bodies also. At the same time, the followers of Jesus who are still living "will be caught up together with them in the clouds to meet the Lord in the air, and so we shall always be with the Lord" (1 Thessalonians 4:17).

What will be the nature of the bodies we'll have during the time we spend in Heaven before the Resurrection? Will they be spiritual or material? There's much room for debate. Many scholars seem to agree that we will be given some type of material, recognizable form—as made evident by the biblical glimpses into glory as well as by the experiences of "everyday" believers who have been given brief looks at the other side.

Randy Alcorn offers his thoughts:

> Given the consistent physical descriptions of the present Heaven and those who dwell there, it seems possible—though this is certainly debatable—that between our earthly life and our bodily resurrection,

God may grant us some physical form that will allow us to function as human beings while in that unnatural state "between bodies," awaiting our resurrection. Just as the intermediate state is a bridge between life of the old Earth and the New Earth, perhaps intermediate bodies, or at least a physical form of some sort, serve as bridges between our present bodies and our resurrected bodies.[50]

Further, our resurrection bodies will be similar to that of Christ's glorified, resurrected body. First John 3:2 tells us, "We know that when He appears, we will be like Him" (1 John 3:2). Having a body "like" the resurrected Christ's will involve having both a spiritual and a physical existence. It will be spiritual in that we might, like Christ, have the almost unimaginable ability to go through walls and doors without opening them, as He did when he appeared in the disciples' midst in spite of closed and locked doors (John 20:19). Consider Dr. Eby's account of standing in a field of flowers during his brief venture beyond life:

> **RICHARD EBY**—I instinctively looked behind me where I had been standing on dozens of blooms. Not one was bent or bruised. Then I watched my feet as I walked a few more steps upon the grass and flowers; they stood upright inside my feet and legs! We simply passed through one another.[51]

Having a body like the risen Christ also means that physically, we will have a form that is recognizable, touchable, and able to eat and drink. Consider how many people saw Him, recognized Him, touched Him, and even ate with Him during the days in between His resurrection and ascension.

As if having a new body isn't enough, it still doesn't tell the complete story of our amazing after-death transformation. We also have a *new mind* to look forward to!

A NEW MIND

"For now we see only a reflection as in a mirror; then we shall see face to face. Now I know in part; then I shall know fully, even as I am fully known" (1 Corinthians 13:12).

Have you ever experienced a moment when, try as you might, you just couldn't understand something? You just can't seem to "get your brain around it," or you joke that you're having "a senior moment." Frustrating, isn't it? However, even the most brilliant minds among us are limited in their knowledge and understanding: "For as the heavens are higher than the earth, So are My ways higher than your ways and My thoughts than your thoughts" (Isaiah 55:9).

For those who place their faith in Jesus Christ, a transformation of the mind begins at the moment we make that life-changing decision to put aside "the old self with its evil practices, and have put on the new self who is being renewed to a true knowledge according to the image of the One who created him" (Colossians 3:9b-10a). That change begins to take place—sometimes in leaps and bounds, other times in indiscernible increments, and sometimes even after steps backwards—over the course of our lives on Earth. It's this change that makes it possible for us to understand "supernatural things," or things of a spiritual nature: "But a natural man does not accept the things of the Spirit of God, for they are foolishness to him; and he cannot understand them, because they are spiritually appraised" (1 Corinthians 2:14). That process of change is instantly completed when we join Him in Heaven. Only after our death will we have a "clear and distinct understanding of divine truths" (Psalm 36:9).[52] That's not to say we will instantly know everything there is to know about everything; that quality of omniscience will always be the Lord's alone. It means, rather that our mental abilities will be operating at their fullest capability, unhindered by the limitations and imperfections imposed on our earthly minds.

A New Heart

A new body, a new mind. These dramatic upgrades don't even represent the best part of the ultimate makeover we can look forward to receiving in Heaven. The most spectacular transformation will take place in our inner being—the heart. The heart, which has harbored that congenital defect called sin throughout all generations, will finally be restored to its original, perfect working order. Like the renewing of our minds begins here on Earth at the moment we decide to follow Christ, a change of heart also begins to occur at that time. We see evidence of this in our day-to-day lives when we do things that would otherwise run against the grain of human nature, such as have patience with those who drive us up the wall, forgive those who deliberately harm us, and love others—even the unlovable.

However, as long as we're alive, "there is sin that still remains in our hearts even though we have become Christians," scholar Wayne Grudem explains. "Once we die and go to be with the Lord, then our sanctification is completed in one sense, for our souls are set free from indwelling sin and are made perfect."[53] Is it possible that this type of liberation of his heart is what David was longing for when he told the Lord that he would only be fulfilled when he would "awake" in the Lord's "likeness" (Psalm 18:15)?

A New Name

Throughout Scripture, great meaning is attached to names. Often, biblical names help describe a person's origin. An example is Moses, who was given his name because his mother "drew him out of the water" (see Exodus 2:10). At other times, names in Scripture reflect a parent's reaction to a child's birth, as with Isaac (see Genesis 21:6), which means "laughter." Most often, however, the highest significance associated with names in the Bible is when they're changed to indicate the beginning of a new direction or a new life. Consider how Abram's name, meaning "high father," was changed to Abraham, meaning "father of a multitude," when the Lord promised to bless all nations through him (Genesis 12:3).

In a sense, "when God changes a name, He is pointing out a new destiny," notes writer Paul Harnett. "It is also called a 'status change.' You might call it a 'spiritual promotion.'"[54]

It seems supremely fitting that when we receive the ultimate upgrade to eternal existence in Heaven, each of us is promised a new name:

> He who has an ear, let him hear what the Spirit says to the churches. To him who overcomes, to him I will give some of the hidden manna, and I will give him a white stone, and a new name written on the stone which no one knows but he who receives it. (Revelation 2:17)

A marvelous mystery is wrapped up in these new names, which only the recipients will understand. (Interestingly, Jesus Himself has a name that only He understands. This is told us in the powerful picture of Christ's Second Advent, described in Revelation 19:12: "His eyes are a flame of fire, and on His head are many [crowns]; and He has a name written on Him which no one knows except Himself.")

Speculating just a bit, when thinking about the thrilling things we can look forward to when we are in our new heavenly bodies, it isn't beyond reason to wonder whether these new names given each believer might be tied somehow to the intimately personal relationship each believer will enjoy with the Lord forever!

Chapter Four

REWARDED!

"For we must all appear before the judgment seat of Christ, that each one may be recompensed for his deeds in the body, according to what he has done, whether good or bad"
(2 Corinthians 5:10).

GEORGE RITCHIE—Something else was present in that room. With the presence of Christ (simultaneously, though I must tell it one by one) also had entered every episode of my entire life. There they were, every thought and event and conversation, as palpable as a series of pictures. There was no first or last, each one was contemporary, each one asked a single question, "What did you do with your time on Earth?"

I looked anxiously among the scenes before me: school, home, scouting and the cross-country track team—a fairly typical boyhood, yet in the light of that Presence it seemed a trivial and irrelevant existence. I searched my mind for good deeds. The Presence asked, "Did you tell anyone about Me?" I answered, "I

> did not have time to do much. I was planning to, then this happened. I am too young to die!"
>
> "No one," the thought was inexpressibly gentle, "is too young to die."[55]

These words, written by George Ritchie about his December 20, 1943, brush with death from double pneumonia, bring up another common denominator of many near-death accounts: The life review. The well-worn expression, "My life flashed before my eyes," springs from real experiences of real people through the ages whose looks into the life to come gave them some sort of a condensed instant replay of their lives.

Even though I personally didn't experience a life review, in putting together this book, we learned of many who did. For example, here's another account, this one from Ricky Randolph, a department of corrections officer and Baptist minister who sustained deadly injuries in a tumble from a mountainside in 1982:

> RICKY RANDOLPH—I held my hands up in front of me and could make out the appearance of a figure sitting on some type of seat. Then, without warning, a voice asked, "What have you done with your life?" The voice penetrated my very being. I had no answer!
>
> Then to my right I saw what seemed to be like a movie, and I was in it. I saw my mother giving birth to me, then I saw my childhood and friends. I saw everything

from my youth up. Before my eyes I saw everything I had ever done!

As my life played out before my very eyes I tried to think of good things I had done. I was raised in church and had been very active in church functions, yet as I pondered on this, I saw a man in his car [who] had [run] out of gas. I had stopped and given him a lift to a local store about a year ago. I had bought him some gas as he had no money and helped him get on his way. I thought to myself, Why am I seeing this? The voice was loud and clear: "You did not hesitate to help this soul, and asked nothing in return. These actions are the essence of good!"

I saw all the people I had hurt as well, and was shown how my actions had set in motion the actions of others. I was stunned! I had never thought of my life having an effect on the actions of my friends, family, and others I had met. I saw the results of all I had done, and I was not pleased at all!

I looked on until the events came to an end. Indeed I had done so little with my life! I had been selfish and cruel in so many ways! I was truly sorry I had done so little. Then again loud and clear I heard the voice speak again, "You must return."[56]

Reports like this are intriguing and exciting, aren't they? They definitely urge us…*dare* us…to consider what we might see on an end-of-life screenplay of our own time on Earth. But, fascinating details value aside, what do we really know about the life review? Or, better put, is the life review scriptural?

The short answer is: "Yes."

Consider these verses:

- "And there is no creature hidden from His sight, but all things are open and laid bare to the eyes of Him with whom we have to do" (Hebrews 4:13).

- "So then each one of us will give an account of himself to God" (Romans 14:12).

- "The conclusion, when all has been heard, is: fear God and keep His commandments, because this applies to every person. For God will bring every act to judgment, everything which is hidden, whether it is good or evil" (Ecclesiastes 12:13–14).

And perhaps nothing in Scripture brings the idea of a life review—an account-giving before the Lord—into clearer focus than the following passage:

> Not everyone who says to Me, "Lord, Lord," will enter the kingdom of heaven, but he who does the will of My Father who is in heaven will enter. Many will say to Me on that day, "Lord, Lord, did we not prophesy in Your name, and in Your name cast out demons, and in Your name perform many miracles?" And then I will

declare to them, "I never knew you; depart from Me, you who practice lawlessness." (Matthew 7:21–23)

Here, Jesus is warning specifically against false teachers and emphasizing the point that it's only a relationship with Him that secures a position of citizenship in His eternal kingdom. But note His reference to a time—"that day"—when those listening to Him will give a personal account of themselves to Him: "Lord, Lord, did we not…?"

Clearly, then, a life review—in the sense that each person at some point will give an account of himself or herself to God—is scriptural. Yet how life reviews described in near-death experiences like the ones we've looked at fit within the framework of what the Bible says is hazy territory, a subject about which I have no trouble admitting that I "see in a mirror dimly" (1 Corinthians 13:12).

So, to help us try to get a handle on the subject, let's back up and take a closer look at what the Bible says about our account-giving to Christ—and at His response.

Moment of Truth

As expressed earlier, the instant the soul leaves the body is when we learn whether our eternity will be spent in Heaven or in Hell.

Those who choose to follow the Lord actually know this fact, with certainty, long before death, at the moment the decision is made. It's critical to realize that there is no way to "earn" heavenly citizenship. It is not a reward for following the Ten Commandments or coloring inside the lines of what society considers good behavior. It is only by accepting God's grace, through faith, that we receive this gift.

At some point—likely not too far into the future, many believe—the Rapture of the church will take place. (Again, that's the moment described in 1 Corinthians 15:51–55 and 1 Thessalonians 4:13–18 when Jesus Christ will return to the visible Heaven above the earth to gather up His followers. The bodies of all the believers throughout the Church Age who have died will be reunited with their spirits and will meet with Christ in the clouds above the earth. All believers who are still alive will join them.) Shortly after the Rapture, all of those individuals will appear before Christ at the judgment seat of Christ. In Scripture, the Greek word used for this judgment is *bema*, a reference to ancient games in which contestants would compete for prizes. The victor in each event was led by the competition's judge to a platform called the bema, where a laurel wreath crown was placed on the winner's head.

REWARDS, NOT JUDGMENT

While the word "judgment" might sound frightening, this isn't an event to be feared in any way, because it won't be a time of sentencing or censure. Just as the winners of the ancient athletic contests received rewards for their accomplishments but did not receive floggings for their failures, this is a judgment that, in a loose sense, might compare to an honors banquet—one in which no one walks out of the door empty-handed.

Let us explain.

When we acknowledge Christ as Lord and set the course of our lives to one that follows Him, we're promised freedom from condemnation (Romans 8:1). All of our sins are "cast…into the depths of the sea" (Micah 7:19) and are completely forgotten (see Hebrew 8:12). So, when it comes to the *sin* of those who love Him, the Lord forgives and forgets.

But, when it comes to the good *activities*—our actions as well as our attitudes—of those who love Him, the Lord never forgets. Psalm 56:8 speaks of a "book" in which the Lord keeps a record of our activity. Also, in Malachi 3:16, we read of the Lord taking special note of the words spoken of Him by those who "fear the Lord and who esteem His name." Our Father, whose "eyes are toward the righteous" at all times (Psalm 34:15), who sees everything we do (Psalm 139:3 and others), and who even understands the motives and intentions of our hearts (Proverbs 16:2; 1 Thessalonians 2:4; Hebrews 4:13; and others), doesn't miss a thing. He wants to reward us for the things we do, say, and even think that honor Him during our time on Earth. As David prayed to the Lord, "And lovingkindness is Yours, O Lord, for You recompense a man according to his work" (Psalm 62:12).

It All Comes Out in the...Fire

The apostle Paul described this judgment process with a vivid illustration (see 1 Corinthians 3:12–15) that goes something like this: Picture a pickup truck into the bed of which everything we do, say, and think over the course of a lifetime is heaped. The things we do, say, and think during our time on Earth that don't bring glory and honor to God, or that don't build up His kingdom, are represented by wood, hay, and stubble piled into the truck bed. This is the ugly part of our payload. In contrast, the things we do, say, and think that have eternal value—things that build up His kingdom and bring Him honor—are represented by gold, silver, diamonds, and rubies strewn across the pile. The beauty of these gems and precious metals is almost sparkly enough to disguise the unsightly yard waste materials in the truck bed. But as the contents of the truck are shoveled onto a blazing bonfire of judgment, the flames quickly find the "wood, hay, and stubble" activities. Of course, they go up in smoke in a matter of minutes. But the precious, imperishable metals and priceless jewels of our good works—the evidence, not the source, of our salvation—remain pure and undamaged, still glimmering among the ashes of the smoldering fire. Those are the activities, words, and thoughts for which we'll be rewarded.

The crowns handed us as rewards are meaningful in that they not only give a nod to our royal inheritance as sons and daughters of the King, but they also point to the laurel wreath crowns awarded to the victorious athletes. The Bible mentions several specific crowns, including:

- The crown of life, given to those who endure trials and suffering (James 1:12; Revelation 2:10)

- The crown of rejoicing, given to those who minister to others for the kingdom of Christ (1 Thessalonians 2:19; Philippians 4:1)

- The crown of righteousness, awarded to those who "long for His appearing" (2 Timothy 4:8)

Many expositors believe the crowns Jesus is described as bringing with Him in Revelation 19:12 are the ones that will be handed out at the bema judgment. All this talk of crowns brings to mind a vivid image reported by Dr. Gerard Landry:

> **GERARD LANDRY**—Then, as if I had eyes all around my head, I saw saints, souls that were in heaven— multitudes. There was no way to count them.... They were "floating" on what appeared to be a crystal mirror or cloud or smoke.... Each person was holding a crown in his or her hand.[57]

Once we receive crowns and other rewards not specifically named in Scripture, we won't be placing them on the mantles of our heavenly mansions for visitors to admire. Instead, Revelation 4:9–11 suggests that because of the Lord's holiness, majesty, and love, we will desire nothing more than to cast our crowns at His feet in worship, returning those rewards to their Source.

WHAT TO MAKE OF THE LIFE REVIEW?

As we've searched the Scriptures to see how the life review common in many near-death experiences might fit into biblical truth, you've no doubt noted something very important: While the account-giving idea is definitely scriptural, these experiences certainly are not in any way describing the judgment seat of Christ. The timing for that simply does not work out because the judgment seat of Christ happens after, not before, the Rapture.

So what, then, do we make of the countless reports of people whose glimpses into Heaven included a detailed look at some of the things they did—or didn't—do for Christ? We can only speculate. Perhaps the answer is so complex that it's far beyond our ability to understand—one of the mysteries referred to in the pages of the Bible that we're not meant to unveil. Or maybe the answer is as simple as this: Perhaps God uses these life reviews as a call to action both for those who experience them and for those who hear of them.

Extraordinary Circumstances

That God might use a life review as one way of speaking to some of His followers isn't a left-field concept. Dr. Charles Stanley, highly respected pastor and author, in teaching about some of the ways God reveals His will, lists a number of methods the Lord uses to communicate with us. He speaks of communication tools such as a restless spirit, a word of wisdom spoken by others, disappointment, and even unanswered prayers. But one of the more intriguing methods of contact Stanley lists is "extraordinary circumstances."

"The Creator can use unusual phenomena to get our attention," he explains. For example, "To attract Moses, God used a burning bush that was not consumed by fire" (Exodus 3:1–22).[58]

A life review, like a burning bush, certainly would qualify as an extraordinary circumstance, wouldn't it? It's an event God can use to secure our undivided attention and then direct us to take action during the time we have remaining on the earth.

"IT'S NOT YOUR TIME (YET)"

We know that the time we have remaining on Earth is limited; we need only visit the local cemetery to see evidence of that. The Bible says that the Lord knows the exact number of our days: "In Your book were written the days that were ordained for me" (Psalm 139:16). So it goes without saying that those who have had near-death experiences did not see death itself because the number of their days hadn't yet come.

"It's not yet your time," a voice told Tony Davis, a young gospel singer, as he teetered between life and death after being shot on the street in front of his wife's workplace. "Tony, your work is not yet done. Go back."[59]

"Jim, I love you...but it is not your time yet. You must go back, for I have many works to do in you."[60] These are the words Jim Sepulveda reports having heard at the conclusion of an indescribably wonderful time in the presence of Jesus following his heart attack.

And Simon Mackrell, in the moments after a fiery crash, vividly recalls a magnificent angel telling him to "return from [to] where you came from." When Mackrell protested, saying that he wanted to stay and be with Jesus, the angel repeated: "The Lord's return is imminent. I have more to do; you are to return [to] where you came."[61]

Each of these people, like Ricky Randolph, whose story we read at the opening of this chapter, came away from their glimpse into life after life with a renewed awareness of opportunities they had missed. They also expressed a revitalized desire to do even more for the Lord in the time they have remaining.

Perhaps the life review, then, is God's way of teaching us to live each day in light of eternity. David prayed along these lines when he asked the Lord to teach him to always be aware of how many days he had to live—the boundary lines around his time on Earth (Psalm 90:12). Jesus highlighted the urgency of our need to spend time in ways worthwhile to His kingdom by stating in John 9:4 that we should do the work of the One who sent us "as long as it is day." And, in his letter to the Ephesians, Paul urged us to make the most of our time—especially in light of the fact that the "days are evil" (5:16).

"God gives us a twenty-four-hour slice of time in which to make the most of every opportunity," says Joni Eareckson Tada, "opportunities that will have eternal repercussions."[62] For those whose life review reflects a decision to love and follow the Lord, those eternal repercussions are indescribably wonderful. But for those whose life review reflects the opposite—an absence of a loving relationship with Jesus Christ—the never-ending outcome is grim indeed.

Chapter Five

DOOMED?

"Then He will also say to those on His left, 'Depart from Me, accursed ones, into the eternal fire which has been prepared for the devil and his angels.' Then they will go away into eternal punishment, but the righteous into eternal life" (Matthew 25:46).

CHRISTINE EASTELL—When my spirit began to leave my body I began to go down into a very deep pit. It is difficult to describe. It was very black and misty. There was no beginning or end, and no sides. I just knew I was in a pit. I kept closing my eyes, and hoping that when I opened them it would all be a bad dream, but nothing changed. It is impossible to find words to describe the fear I felt. I was desperate to get out. When I saw what I thought was a small opening I began to claw desperately. But the more I tried to get to this opening, the more distant it became. It was an impossible situation.[63]

It isn't usually a good writing strategy to begin a chapter by warning that its content promises to be just awful. Unfortunately, that's the way this one begins, because it isn't realistic to offer a glimpse into the glories of Heaven without considering the sobering reality of the horrors of the alternative eternal destination, Hell.

The very idea of a place of eternal punishment is so off-putting, in fact, that fewer and fewer people these days even believe Hell is real.

"For more and more Americans, hell is a myth," according to a survey released by the Pew Forum on Religion and Public Life in 2008. "Just 59 percent of 35,000 respondents said they believe in a hell 'where people who have led bad lives, and die without being sorry, are eternally punished.'" That's down from the 71 percent who said they believed in hell in a 2001 Gallup survey. And it is lower than the 74 percent who said they believe in heaven in the recent Pew poll.[64]

Believing that Hell exists, however, comes easily to at least one group of people—those who have had hellish encounters in a life-after-death realm. For example, Dr. Don Whitaker, a professed atheist who was not expected to survive a deadly pancreatic disease, has no trouble saying he believes that Hell is real. He describes the horrific details of the place he saw while fighting for his life:

DON WHITAKER—There are people that talk about a light, or floating above, a feeling of warmth or love. I didn't feel any of that. I felt none of that. I felt untold terror.... I knew that if I went all the way, if I slipped all the way, I would never get back. In my being of beings I knew that. So I fought all night long.[65]

Neither does Christine Eastell find it hard to think of Hell as an actual place after experiencing what she described at the opening of this chapter. She endured the terrifying ordeal after receiving life-threatening injuries in a head-on collision.

CHRISTINE EASTELL—When my spirit began to leave my body, I began to go down into a very deep pit.... It was very black and misty. There was no beginning or end, and no sides.... I kept closing my eyes, and hoping that when I opened them it would all be a bad dream, but nothing changed. It is impossible to find words to describe the fear I felt.

DANGEROUS LIES

Because the topic of Hell is such a sensational one, speculation about it abounds—and that has led to some commonly held beliefs about it that are gravely wrong. For example, some people say they'd actually rather go to Hell than to Heaven when they die. Like the lyrics from the 1977 Billy Joel song suggest, they would "rather laugh with the sinners than cry with the saints, because the sinners are much more fun." After all, they reason, Hell's the place where the fun-lovers get together and party—and that seems much more appealing than the boring alternative of wearing white robes, plucking harps, and hanging out with the "church people."[66]

Others concede that Hell probably is a terrible place, and that it isn't necessarily where they would want to spend eternity. But then they venture onto the thin-ice thinking that says that nobody who's even marginally decent will go there.

"Today, there is an almost universal heresy," observes author Gary Stearman in his book *Time Travelers*. "It says that all people, regardless of belief, are bound for heaven. It teaches that there are many pathways to the Kingdom of Heaven."[67] This attitude not only holds that there are many roads that bypass Hell to lead just about anyone—except maybe murderers, child molesters, and rapists—straight to Heaven, but that it's because God is far too loving to send anyone to Hell.

Of course, none of these lines of reasoning are based on any kind of biblical truth. In fact, they're as far off-base as the cartoonish image of the red Spandex-wearing Satan reigning over Hell with a pitchfork for a scepter. The only dependable way to separate fiction from the facts is by beginning and ending any research with Jesus' own words about the subject.

DANGEROUS TRUTHS

"There is no doctrine which I would more willingly remove from Christianity than this (hell) if it lay in my power. But it has the full support of Scripture and, especially, of our Lord's own words; it has always been held by Christendom; and has the support of reason."

C. S. Lewis[68]

To accomplish His goal of seeking out and saving those who don't know Him from the certain, eternal death (the consequences, or "wages" of sin spoken of in Romans 6:23) that would result from refusing to accept His gift of eternal life, Jesus spoke often about Heaven. But He taught even more frequently about Hell.

"[Jesus] motivated loving actions with the hope of reward in heaven, and he motivated radical purity with the fear of hell," notes John Piper. "For Jesus, a profound desire for heaven and fear of hell were practical, daily parts of living a glad and holy life."[69]

And you can be sure that when Jesus broached the subject of Hell, He held nothing back, describing it as the opposite of Heaven in every aspect.

Whenever Jesus described hell, He was never flippant or dismissive. He used vivid, terrifying terms to describe the final destination of sinners, shocking and scaring His audiences with frighteningly graphic metaphors. Hell is a place so bad that you should be willing to cut off sensitive, irreplaceable parts of your body to avoid it (Matthew 5:29–30); even martyrdom would be worth avoiding the torment of hell (Matthew 10:28). He always presented hell as a *horrific* place of intolerable suffering.[70]

Here are just a few of the ways Christ has described the terrors of Hell:

Furnace of Fire

Possibly one of the most common images associated with Hell is fire. Unlike much of the off-based thinking going around about that place, these images are based on truth. In Matthew 13:42 and 50, Jesus likened Hell to a "furnace of fire," where the flames are unquenchable (see Mark 9:48–49). And He pulled no punches about the reality of Hell in the story of the rich man sentenced to Hell who cried out for a drop of water to "cool off my tongue; for I am in agony in this flame" (Luke 16:19–31).

A frightening preview of a fiery scenario is precisely what Ronald Reagan (*not* the president), a drug-addicted criminal, saw as he peered into a "volcanic opening" following severe injuries he received during a violent brawl:

RONALD REAGAN—As I was looking down…I saw fire, smoke and people inside of this burning place. They were screaming and crying, they were burning, but they weren't burning up, they weren't being consumed. Then I began moving downward into this opening.[71]

Certainly the worst part about this "furnace of fire" is that it not only provides a violent and disturbing backdrop for Hell's residents (especially when contrasted against the beauty and perfection of Heaven), but the burns it causes inflict the worst kind of pain imaginable. That makes it highly likely that "laughing with the sinners" is a never-gonna-happen activity there. No one could possibly laugh while enduring that kind of agony.

Outer Darkness

Heaven, as we'll discuss in a later chapter, is a place of incredible light and beauty. But Hell, we learn from Jesus' words in Matthew 8:12 and 22:13, is a place of "outer darkness," the kind of empty blackness that might be like what was seen by Angie Fenimore, a wife and mother who became suicidal following a series of upsetting events and circumstances in her life. She said that she was "immersed in darkness" after trying to end her own life; then her eyes "seemed to adjust." She continued:

> **ANGIE FENIMORE**—I could see clearly even though there was no light. The darkness continued in all directions and seemed to have no end, but it wasn't just blackness, it was an endless void, an absence of light. It was completely enveloping.[72]

There's a good explanation for that kind of immense, never-ending darkness. God is light (1 John 1:5) and is referred to as the Father of lights (James 1:17). So it makes sense that Hell, the place farthest removed from Him and His presence, would be marked by an absence of light.

Along with the nonexistence of light, the darkness also signifies the "loneliness, insecurity, [and] the sense of being lost and disoriented."[73] Angie Fenimore experienced a taste of that, too:

> **ANGIE FENIMORE**—Worse was my growing sense of complete aloneness. Even hearing the brunt of someone's anger, however unpleasant, is a form of tangible connection. But in this empty world, where no connections could be made, the solitude was terrifying.[74]

Those who are in the "I'd rather laugh with the sinners than cry with the saints" camp should see the darkness and isolation as a wake-up call: There won't be any kind of social life or meaningful interactions in Hell.

Weeping and Gnashing of Teeth

In stark contrast to Heaven as a place of physical, spiritual, and emotional *restoration*, Jesus makes it clear that Hell is a place of physical, spiritual, and emotional *destruction*. He used the phrase "weeping and gnashing of teeth" several times to convey this thought (see Matthew 8:12 and Luke 13:28, for example). The "weeping" suggests sorrow and grief (the emotional agony of the lost in Hell), and "gnashing," or "grinding of one's teeth[,] speaks of pain (physical agony in hell)."[75] This might be like what Christine Eastell observed during her brush with death:

> **CHRISTINE EASTELL**—All around there were people, just ordinary people. They were in deep pain and despair, and they seemed to be tormented by an enormous sense of guilt, which was reflected in their faces. It is so difficult to describe the depth of despair that was present in that place. If you could put all the pain, hurt, and despair in the world together, then that was what I sensed in that place. I was far more aware of the depth of this despair than I was of the people.[76]

As one blogger puts it:

> Hell is not a dark, comfortable pub where you can hang out with friends and talk about the meaning of life (or hell) throughout the ages. Nor is hell some kind of everlasting rave, thumping with house music

and lit with glow sticks. Hell is no party. Hell is not what you make it…. It is a dark, endless, joyless, place of judgment.[77]

Eternal

Finally, as we consider this sampling of the realities Jesus taught about Hell, we must understand one thing as clearly as possible: It's a forever destination. Calling it "eternal punishment" (Matthew 25:46), He made it clear that no one ever has the option of leaving. As John MacArthur explains:

> Punishment in hell is defined by the word *aionios*, which is the word "eternal" or "everlasting." There are people who would like to redefine that word *aionios* and say, "Well, it doesn't really mean forever." But if you do that with hell, you've just done it with heaven, because the same word is used to describe both. If there is not an everlasting hell, then there is not an everlasting heaven. And I'll go one beyond that. The same word is used to describe God. And so if there is not an everlasting hell, then there is not an everlasting heaven, nor is there an everlasting God. It is clear that God is eternal; and, therefore, that heaven is eternal, and so is hell.[78]

While professional skydiver Mickey Robinson was fighting to survive after a plane crash, his heart stopped and he had a "life-changing experience" that left no doubt in his mind that Hell would be an eternal destination:

MICKEY ROBINSON—In an instant, the physical world vanished and my inner man came out of my physical body. I was no longer in the hospital room—I had entered into the realm of the spirit....

A great darkness began to surround me, and I saw this was actually a point of separation. Coming through the closing space was a beam of the purest whitest light I had ever seen. The doorway began closing faster and faster. The meaning of this separation became illuminated to me. I knew that if this door would close completely, I would be cut off for all eternity from this light.

I experienced a deep hopelessness and horror. Separation is hopelessness! Eternal separation is a torment beyond belief. I want you to know there is a place established somewhere that is eternal separation. I was permitted to not only see, but to experience the feeling of what it would be like to be in this eternal separation.[79]

Avoiding our
"Default Destination"

As chilling as the thought of spending forever in a place like this is, Randy Alcorn bluntly refers to Hell as our "default destination" because of the simple and profound fact that we have all "sinned and fall short" of the standards it takes to enter God's holy presence.[80] Only by accepting Jesus' payment for our sins on the cross and establishing a trusting, loving relationship with Him can we receive the new standing in God's eyes that makes us pure enough for Him to call us family.

So, as difficult (and unpopular) an idea as it may be to grasp, we know that a loving God can and must judge some people worthy of spending eternity in Hell, rather than Heaven. That truth is emphasized throughout the pages of Scripture, and it is illustrated by the one characteristic shared by those whose near-death experiences we've read about in this chapter: the absence of a personal relationship with Jesus Christ.

Professed atheist Don Whitaker, for example, "believed in the power of the universe" and had no need whatsoever for God or Jesus Christ. He explains:

> **DON WHITAKER**—I believed in the power of the universe because I've seen it. As a physician, I've dealt with life and death. I believed in something, but don't talk to me about God. And surely don't talk to me

about resurrection, virgin birth or these type of things because I am in research and science.

Likewise, Angie Fenimore had never trusted Christ, saying she had always "doubted His existence" and had "questioned the authenticity of the Scriptures because what they claimed seemed too good to be true."

On the other hand, Mickey Robinson and Christine Eastell didn't have such pronounced anti-God or anti-Jesus positions. In fact, Robinson said that when he was young, he had gone to church every Sunday and had been "endowed with a knowledge of God" before drifting away from the faith lifestyle of his Roman Catholic upbringing. And Christine Eastell says, "I had thought I was a Christian, but I had not committed my life to Jesus."

Robinson and Eastell are the type of people who bring to mind Jesus' words in Matthew 7: 21–23:

> Not everyone who says to Me, "Lord, Lord," will enter the kingdom of heaven, but he who does the will of My Father who is in heaven will enter. Many will say to Me on that day, "Lord, Lord, did we not prophesy in Your name, and in Your name cast out demons, and in Your name perform many miracles?" And then I will declare to them, "I never knew you; depart from Me, you who practice lawlessness."

"Surely there are no more serious words for religious people to hear than these," says John MacArthur about that passage of Scripture. "No more serious words for people who profess Christianity than these because our Lord says there will not be a few but many who are mistaken about their future destiny. He points out…the folly of empty words, and then the tragedy of empty hearts…empty words coming from empty hearts."[81]

Either way—whether deliberately and openly opposing the Lord or by aimlessly remaining uncommitted to Him—Jesus makes it clear that Hell is the only possible after-life destiny for those who die without trusting Him as their Lord and Savior.

No Second Chances

Given their beliefs and the nature of what they saw, smelled, heard, tasted, and felt during their brushes with death, then, it's an understatement to say that the people we've heard from in this chapter were thrilled to learn their experiences were "near-death" and not "death" itself. The terror they endured was so awful and so real that they couldn't wait to return to their lives on Earth. When they did regain consciousness, they were intensely determined to make a single, dramatic change in their lives: They decided to follow rather than reject Jesus Christ, entrusting their lives to His care both on Earth and into eternity.

For example, Mickey Robinson reports undergoing a "repentance process" as he lay dying:

> **MICKEY ROBINSON**—As I was lying there, very injured, and nearly dead, I cried out, "God. I am sorry! Please give me another chance!" Many times I went through the swinging doors into surgery, not knowing if I would wake up, and this knowledge started something inside me. I did not know how to pray, but I begged God for forgiveness.[82]

Ronald Reagan likewise made that critical decision:

> **RONALD REAGAN**—What could I do? There I was in hell, with Satan, and in total despair. I had thought I was a Christian, but I had not committed my life to Jesus.
>
> At that point I thought, "Lord, please rescue me." I prayed for forgiveness, and I remember falling on my knees pleading with Him to forgive me.... Then I stayed there, because I could not do anything else. But, praise God, Satan is a defeated enemy.[83]

Reagan says he believes his life was spared for one reason only: "To tell others about the place that I had seen, and the hope of Jesus Christ to save mankind from this terrible fate."[84]

The stories of these people and the accounts from many others have "happy endings." They did not die before they had a chance to trust the Lord with their lives and their eternal future. However, had the flatlines on their heart monitors remained perfectly horizontal and still, their stories would have ended much differently. They wouldn't have had a chance to make those decisions to follow Jesus; they would have permanently entered "eternal destruction" and been sentenced forever to an existence "away from the presence of the Lord and from the glory of his power" (1 Thessalonians 1:9).

Although most people would like to believe that everyone gets some kind of a second chance after they die if they don't like where they end up, no do-overs are given once one's soul leaves his or her body. If Hell is, in fact, a person's final destination, he or she "will forever be hopeless, helpless, and powerless."[85] That's why it's critical to "choose for yourselves today"—not tomorrow, or next year, or after college, or after retirement—"whom you will serve" (Joshua 24:15). The Lord loves us and doesn't want any of us to go to Hell, we're told in 2 Peter 3:9. He wants us to be in Heaven with Him.

He wants that so much that He's already prepared a home for us there.

Chapter Six

HOME!

"In My Father's house are many dwelling places; if it were not so, I would have told you; for I go to prepare a place for you. If I go and prepare a place for you, I will come again and receive you to Myself, that where I am, there you may be also"
(John 14:2–3).

"For our citizenship is in heaven, from which also we eagerly wait for a Savior, the Lord Jesus Christ" (Philippians 3:20).

"The Bible says this world is not our final home— but we do have one, and that is heaven."

Billy Graham[86]

A recent poll asked for a brief answer to the question, "What's the first thing that comes to mind when you hear the word

'Heaven'?" A one-word response cropped up far more than any others: *Home.*

Although it was, granted, an unscientific method of gathering information (a quick survey among a group of friends), it did reveal a telling truth: We're mostly a homesick bunch of folks who are looking forward to Heaven with as much longing and excitement as a college student might look forward to home near the end of a long semester of crowded, noisy, and not-so-comfy dorm life. (Ramen noodles lose their appeal once your mouth starts watering for Mom's pot roast and gravy!)

A sense of being finally and completely at home is yet another common theme that punctuates many of those who have experienced a brush with death.

SIMON MACKRELL—I put my arms out pointing into the city and said, "I am home."[87]

BORIS PILIPSHUK—When I entered into the city through the gates, I stood in admiration.... I touched the walls and entered some houses, observing everything. I did not ask the angels where I was to go from here. I seemed to know the way. I was overcome with such a feeling as if I was in a place of my own.[88]

The fact that we would find the home-like atmosphere of Heaven to be such a relief raises a puzzling question: If God Himself spoke this amazing planet into existence, why are we already scanning the horizon for a better place? Why don't we feel completely at home, here in the surroundings that were custom made for us? After all, we learn from the book of Genesis that when the Lord created the world, it was, "in a sense…the first-ever tabernacle, or dwelling place of God [on earth], because that's where God, Adam, and Eve lived in pristine splendor and perfect harmony."[89]

Pristine splendor…perfect harmony with God and each other. Who could want anything more? No one! No one, that is, until the first-ever bride decided to listen to the serpent's beguiling lies and convince her newlywed husband to join her in breaking God's one rule about not eating the fruit from a particular tree. "When they did, their sin shattered their fellowship and intimacy with God, because it is impossible for holiness, or perfection, to coexist with unholiness, or imperfection."[90]

That act of rebellion was a real game-changer, infecting the human race for every generation to follow with a tendency to sin. "The door was now opened wide for people to begin making their own rules and letting their own selfish desires guide their decisions," observes Bible scholar and author Larry Richards. "People are not sinners because they do wrong, but *choose wrong* because they are sinners."[91] This explains how people created in God's image could "produce a race marred by crime, injustice, hatred, and war."[92] Thousands of years and many generations later, the human race continues to live out the legacy of sin that was decisively—defiantly—established by our ancestors on that ancient day when the world was new.

However…because God created people for His pleasure, fellowship, and love, as well as to bring glory to Himself, He provided a way for us to reenter His presence. That was accomplished through a highly symbolic and deeply meaningful system of sacrifice and worship, which culminated in the birth, ministry, death, resurrection, and ascension of Christ, the sacrificial lamb without any flaws who "bore our sins in His body on the cross, so that we might die to sin and live to righteousness"(1 Peter 2:24).

The minute we recognize Jesus for who He is and what He did and choose to follow Him, we're immediately adopted into His family, securing instant citizenship in Heaven (see Ephesians 1:5 and Philippians 3:20). The Holy Spirit moves into our hearts and transformation begins.

The changes happen in varying degrees for different people. At first, we may stop thinking, speaking, or acting the same as we did before. We may notice that our motives, our goals, and even our desires are taking on a different shape. We realize we've made an about face on the "broad way" the world is traveling (which, the Bible says, happens to lead straight toward destruction) and begin heading in the opposite direction, through the "narrow gate" (Matthew 7:13–14). As we stride down this new path, we soon notice that the shoes we were wearing on the old road no longer fit, reminding us with each blistering step that, just as Peter said, we're not designed for the here and now; we're just passing through it as "aliens and strangers" (1 Peter 2:11).

RUNNING INTO TROUBLE
ON THE WAY HOME

Heaven, the dwelling place of God, then, becomes our native land, our new hometown, the place we program into the GPS. We long for it as passionately as we would if we had physically been born there—and even more during those times when, as Jesus promised, we meet with inevitable trouble (John 16:33). That trouble comes in many forms—from stress, fatigue, busyness, and opposition to illness, financial peril, overwhelming temptations, and outright violence.

"Pressing forward, sometimes falteringly, there are days when discouragement sets in and I feel I'm wandering around in circles," says Jim Palmer in his book, *Divine Nobodies*, expressing a sense that most of us can easily identify with. "I think I understand Peter's description of being 'aliens and strangers in the world' and often feel this way even among church people."[93]

The Up Side of Trouble

While acute homesickness is not a great feeling, we can take comfort in the fact that this discontentment with the present world and longing for the next is evidence of a healthy spiritual life. Trouble has a way of chasing us into the arms of the Lord more frequently, and of pressing us into Him with more urgency. When we're in trouble, we, like David, know where our help comes from (see Psalm 121:2); we know who can give us what we need to get through difficult days. It was trouble that visited Rev. Billy Graham's wife, Ruth Bell Graham, in the form of intense homesickness along with her physical illness when she was just thirteen and living in a girls' dormitory in a boarding school in Pyong Yang, China, that compelled her to find comfort in God's Word:

> The homesickness settled in unmercifully. The days she could somehow manage. It was the nights that became unbearable. Burying her head in her pillow, she tried not to disturb her sleeping roommates.
>
> Night after night, week after week, she cried herself to sleep, silently, miserably.
>
> A few weeks later, Ruth became sick and was sent to the infirmary for several days. She propped herself up on her pillows and spent the entire time reading the Psalms, all 150 of them. The tiny corner room in the infirmary building still holds warm memories for Ruth because of the strength she received from those timeless, timely passages.[94]

The trouble we have in this world also keeps our eyes focused on the prize. "Genuine spirituality cannot live long without an attitude that is homesick for Heaven, that lives with eternity's values in view, that eagerly awaits Jesus' return, that anticipates the day when Christ himself will 'bring everything under his control,' and 'will transform our lowly bodies to be like his glorious body (Philippians 3:21),'" says D. A. Carson.[95] Maybe this is why Paul urged us to keep our eyes always fixed on Jesus. And maybe it's why Jesus' straightforward advice for combating the troubles we experience as children of God living in a land governed by the god of this world, Satan, is to rely on the fact that, even now, the One who was a carpenter by trade is preparing a place for us in Heaven (John 14:1–2).

…Which brings our topic back home.

THE SPECS OF A SPECTACULAR HOME

It's no secret that our homes are important to us. Next to the word "mom," "home" might be a strong contender for the most emotion-packed word in the English language. Americans spend countless time and money fixing up, adding on, and planting new shrubs in order to improve the curb appeal of their digs. Even as the real estate boom turned into a housing bust, the phenomenon dubbed "house lust" keeps the momentum to buy, sell, rent, and upgrade moving full speed ahead in the quest to live in the ultimate dream home.

But truth be told, no matter how high the ceilings in the living room, how well-suited for entertaining the kitchen, how spacious the walk-in closets, or how expensive the finishes and hardware, no house, tepee, or motor home on Earth can match the magnificence of our heavenly one. Again, we can't possibly know every detail about the place the woodworker from Galilee is even now custom crafting for us in Heaven, but we can enjoy a look at some of the tantalizing details.

A Safe Home

> "For You alone, O LORD, make me to dwell in safety"
> (Psalm 4:8b).

As mentioned earlier, we're guaranteed to encounter trouble in this life. Not to sound paranoid or pessimistic, but even day-to-day living can be a dangerous business, with threats to the well-being of our loved ones and ourselves seemingly always on the brink of happening. With Satan as the acknowledged prince of this world, the souls of God's followers are never in jeopardy, but our physical and emotional well-being are constantly at risk of falling to the consequences of living in a foreign country under an evil, despotic leader. We often need to lock our doors against intruders, keep our fingers positioned over the "panic" button on our key fobs in parking lots at night, and always be careful not to wander into dangerous parts of town. We have to make a deliberate effort to stay safe.

But if operative words when speaking about life on this planet include "troubling" and "dangerous," a key word describing Heaven is just the opposite: "safety." In Heaven, as we go about our day-to-day living, we'll never need deadbolt locks, panic buttons, or knowledge of where the "bad part of town" is located, because no part of that place is a bad part!

Further, we're told in Revelation 21:12 that the heavenly city is securely surrounded by a "great and high wall"—perhaps something similar to what Jim Wilhelm, who accidentally ingested wasp poison, says about what he saw on the other side:

> JIM WILHELM—Looking to my right where the river came from, there was a beautiful stone-built wall that was about one-half mile high. It was about 200 yards away from where I was standing by the river....
>
> Behind the heavenly wall there were people talking, and people worshiping.... I approached the wall but could not see inside of it.[96]

Just to be clear: A wall is not necessary in Heaven as a defense against intruders. Rather, it serves as a beautiful picture of God's protection of His people. The structure, which is some 200 feet thick, "gives the city perimeters (this is no cosmic nirvana) and shows us that some will be excluded from the city (only the righteous can enter)."[97]

"The strong implication is that those inside will be safe...forever!" notes Anne Graham Lotz. "No more missiles or guns in schools or terrorists or suicide bombers or drive-by shootings or ethnic cleansings or tornadoes or tsunamis or earthquakes tremors or rapes or robberies or home invasions…make your own list."[98]

Further upping the "safety rating" of Heaven, Revelation 21:12 states that angelic sentries will be posted at each of twelve gates in the walls—reminiscent of the cherubim who stood guard at the entrance to the Garden of Eden (Genesis 3:24). Imagine having an eternal destiny where our security is ensured by the watchful care of God and His angels!

A Spacious Home

"He brought me out into a spacious place" (Psalm 18:19, NIV).

Certainly the wear and tear of life in this world is intensified by the people, pressures, and problems constantly crowding in. With a global population of well over 7 billion that is growing at a rate of 1.096 percent a year, it seems like space is quickly running out![99, 100] "I feel like the walls are closing in on me" is a common refrain from the world-weary pilgrim who is homesick for the piece of heavenly real estate that has his or her name on the mailbox. Isn't it refreshing to know that Heaven is described as a great big place—with plenty of room to stretch out and be comfortable?

The heavenly city measures approximately 1,500 miles by 1,500 miles by 1,500 miles.… The eternal city is so huge that it would measure approximately the distance from Canada to Mexico, and from the Atlantic Ocean to the Rockies. That is a surface area of 2.25 million square miles (by comparison, London is only 621 square miles). Put another way, the ground level area of the city will be 15,000 times that of London.

The city is tall enough that from the earth's surface it would reach about one-twentieth of the way to the moon. If the city has stories, each being twelve feet high, then the city would have 600,000 stories. That is huge!...

Someone calculated that if this structure is cube-shaped, it would allow for 20 billion residents, each having his or her own private 75-acre cube. If each residence were smaller, then there is room to accommodate 100 thousand billion people. Even then, plenty of room is left over for parks, streets, and other things you would see in any normal city.[101]

A Busy Home

It's sad to say that many don't think of Heaven very highly. They have a not-so-glowing picture of it for two primary reasons: First, you must die to get there; second, the thought of sitting around for all of eternity on a cloud, strumming a harp, is anything but appealing. However, the God who designed us as beings in motion—with physical, mental, and emotional energy to burn—doesn't intend for us to remain idle for all eternity. "The heaven of all spiritual natures is not idleness," states Alexander

Maclaren. "Man's delight is activity.... The joys of heaven are not the joys of passive contemplation, of dreamy remembrance, of perfect repose; but they are described thus, 'They rest not day nor night.' His servants serve Him, and see His face."[102]

Indeed, "Heaven is a city of incredible activity," notes Todd Strandberg of the Rapture Ready website. "Its splendor surpasses the glitter of Las Vegas, the hustle and bustle of New York City, and the political authority of Washington, DC."

Everything that can be gleaned from the Bible concerning the topic indicates that we'll not only *not* be lounging around in our golden pjs, but that we'll have plenty of opportunities to put our purpose and passion to work carrying on the business of the heavenly kingdom.

What is some of that kingdom work we'll be doing?

Here are a few possibilities:

- **Learning**—The longer we live, the more we understand how little we really know. Questions about subjects ranging from the meaning of life and human relationships to science and the whys of the way things work out can often perplex us to the point of frustration. But imagine finally getting to find out the answers to those questions you've always had! Pointing to 1 Corinthians 13:12, in which Paul stated that we will "know fully" in Heaven what we only "know in part" on Earth, Bible scholar Bob Deffinbaugh suggests that learning will be one focus of our attention in Heaven. "Part of the joy of heaven for me," he says, "will be sitting at the feet of our Lord, learning the correct interpretation of many passages which I do not understand, as well as the meaning of some passages I thought I did understand."[103] Our fellowship with the One who is wisdom itself will offer us the opportunity to enjoy the thrill of learning for all eternity!

- **We'll Be Leading.** As sons and daughters of the King, "fellow heirs with Christ" (Romans 8:17), our heavenly inheritance includes responsibilities as well as riches. "He who overcomes," Jesus promises, "I will grant to him to sit down with Me on My throne, as I also overcame and sat down with My Father on His throne." (Revelation 3:21; see also 2 Timothy 2:12). Our duties will include having authority "over the nations" (see Revelation 2:26; 5:10; 20:6; 22:5) and judging the angels: "Do you not know that the saints will judge the world? If the world is judged by you, are you not competent to constitute the smallest law courts? Do you not know that we will judge angels? How much more matters of this life?" (1 Corinthians 6:2–3).

How is it that we rate such a high position of responsibility and authority in the heavenly kingdom?

When the Lord created the earth and placed the first couple in it, His good plan was for mankind to be in charge of His creation (see Genesis 1:26–28). "Man's right to rule over God's creation is linked with Adam being made in the image of God," Michael Vlach says in his blog on TheologicalStudies.org. "Being made in the image of God means that man is created to represent God over the creation. He is to rule over God's creation for the glory of God."[104]

Yet when mankind veered off the good course designed by God, that reign over the earth was disrupted and distorted. Hebrews 2:5–8 offers a promise that this God-ordained leadership will be fully restored in Heaven:

> For He did not subject to angels the world to come, concerning which we are speaking. But one has testified somewhere, saying, "What is man, that You remember him? Or the son of man, that You are concerned about him? You have made him for a little while lower than the angels; You have crowned him with glory and honor, and have appointed him over the works of Your hands; You have put all things in subjection under his feet."

"When the author of Hebrews says that we do 'not yet' see everything in subjection to man (Hebrews 2:8), he implies that eventually all things will be subject to us, under the kingship of the man Christ Jesus," says Wayne Grudem. "This will fulfill God's original plan to have everything in the world subject to the human beings that he had made."[105]

- **Worshiping.** In his account of what happened to him as he approached what seemed to be certain death, Boris Pilipshuk describes feeling an "overwhelming urge" to drop to his knees in worship. There's a solid correlation between his experience and what the Bible says we can expect to do in Heaven.

For many of us walking the earth, our actions don't always match our intentions when it comes to worshiping our Lord. Because of commitments and calendars, only rarely do we have or make the chance to offer praise and thanksgiving to the Lord through the week. And even the worship we participate in on the one day set aside for that singular purpose is often derailed. "A.W. Tozer once called worship the 'missing jewel' of the modern church," notes David Jeremiah, who suggests that "many Christians never experience the joy of worshipping God in spirit and truth."[106] On Sunday mornings, distractions ranging from a racing mind and a hard pew to displeasure with the song choice and thoughts of picking up some fried chicken on the way home from church can keep our gaze locked at eye level rather than directed upward on our Creator and Savior. But imagine for a moment having those disrupted thoughts and grumbling stomachs erased from the picture. Then consider being seated not in a sanctuary but in the throne room of God Himself.

Such a scenario is exactly what the apostle John was allowed to see when he was given a glimpse through the door to Heaven. "What John sees on the other side of that door is massive worship taking place," says David Jeremiah.[107] Here's part of John's description of that sight:

> And when the living creatures give glory and honor and thanks to Him who sits on the throne, to Him who lives forever and ever, the twenty-four elders will fall down before Him who sits on the throne, and will worship Him who lives forever and ever, and will cast their crowns before the throne, saying,
>
> "Worthy are You, our Lord and our God, to receive glory and honor and power; for You created all things, and because of Your will they existed, and were created." (Revelation 4:9–11)

"We are going to be part of that great worship experience where forever we bring honor and glory to our God," says Jeremiah. "It won't be something we are made to do, it will be something that grows out of the very nature of who we are in Christ. We will find worship to be the most joyous experience we have ever known."[108]

The Bible makes it clear that music will play a big part of this worship, and in fact hearing the praise music of Heaven is among the highlights of many accounts from those who have had brushes with death. In his bump against eternity following a collision between his car and a tractor-trailer rig, Don Piper recalls hearing "literally thousands of praise songs." Betty Malz describes hearing voices that "were melodious, harmonious, [and] blending in chorus," and she describes not only hearing the beautiful music, but adding her voice to the chorus:

> **BETTY MALZ**—I have always had a girl's body, but a low, "boy's," voice. Suddenly I realized I was singing the way I had always wanted to…in high, clear tones…. [Then] the unseen voices picked up a new chorus. The voices not only burst forth in more than four parts, but they were in different languages. I was awed by the richness and perfect blending of the words—and I could understand them![109]

And Richard Eby reports the following:

> **RICHARD EBY**—I had been aware of the most beautiful, melodious, angelic background music that the ear of man can perceive…. It was truly a new song, such as St. John must have heard from Patmos. Not instrumental, not vocal, not mathematical, not earthly. It originated from no one point—neither from the sky nor the ground. Just as was true of the light, the music emerged, apparently, from everything and every place. It had no beat—was neither major nor minor—and had no tempo. (In eternity, how could

it have "time"?) No earthly adjectives describe its angelic quality. Poets have said "music of the spheres." God has said, "A new song will I give them." I heard it—it had to be His composition—every note. Hallelujah! Music by Jesus. No wonder the cherubim and seraphim and multitudes sing around His throne![110]

With all this talk of worship, it's easy to picture throngs of Heaven's inhabitants gathering in what we envision as a traditional Jewish temple—much like the magnificent one Solomon built during his reign. However, there will not be a temple in Heaven. There will be no need. "Here in the new Jerusalem," W. A. Criswell explains, "in the home where the redeemed shall live, a great temple is not needed because the redeemed shall live in the presence of God himself, and they shall look directly into the face of the Almighty with no veil to separate them from him."[111] He explains that the "unseen presence of God" believers on Earth experience "meant that we walked by faith and not by sight. Now sight is added to the glory of heaven."[112]

A Restful Home

> "And I heard a voice from heaven, saying, 'Write, "Blessed are the dead who die in the Lord from now on!"' 'Yes,' says the Spirit, 'so that they may rest from their labors, for their deeds follow with them'" (Revelation 14:13).

Even a good night's sleep doesn't ensure that we won't wake up feeling tired. True rest—the kind that moves beyond getting enough z's after a hard day of work—involves freedom not only from physical exertion but from mental, emotional, and spiritual strain as well. And it's a hard commodity to come by. Calling "rest" "too rich a syllable for this unstable earth," nineteenth-century preacher Charles Spurgeon points out why it's hard for us to get any good rest: "Can there ever be rest for the race who were driven out of Paradise to till the ground from where they were taken and to eat bread in the sweat of their face?"[113] In other words, the fact that we're living in a fallen world with a fallen nature makes true rest impossible—apart from having a close and trusting relationship with God. Even then, the rest offered by the Lord to those who trust Him, much like other aspects of our spiritual growth, tends to come in fits and starts.

But when we get to Heaven, all that will change. Rather than feeling sleep-deprived as many of our days here find us, we will enter the type of tranquility and rest the Bible speaks of as God's rest. The activities we engage in—all that learning, leading, worshiping, and other endeavors—will energize rather than exhaust us.

"Heaven is the earthly life of a believer glorified and perfected," says Maclaren. "If here we by faith enter into the beginning of rest, yonder through death with faith, we shall enter into the perfection of it…Rest in heaven—rest in God!"[114]

A Magnificent Home

The descriptions of Heaven offered in the Bible seem beyond our wildest imagination. Neither the word "magnificent" nor any other superlative comes close to summing up its splendor. But to get at least an inkling of what we might expect in Heaven, we can look at a few snapshots of its characteristics described in the Bible and by those who seem to have had glimpses of that place.

New Jerusalem: A Real City—It's easy to slip into the mindset that Heaven is some kind of nebulous existence that resembles nothing we're used to in everyday life. Yet the first snapshot we see as we piece together what Heaven might be like is that it is consistently described as a city. Most scholars agree that the image conveyed by that word shouldn't be too different than the way we're used to thinking of cities. The heavenly city, the New Jerusalem, clearly will be a tangible, working metropolis—complete with things like structures, dwelling places, and streets. Serving as the ideal surroundings for our brand-new bodies, this place will be absent all the unpleasant elements like pollution, overcrowding, and noise typically found in earthly urban centers. Instead, it will be pristine and peaceful.

There was certainly no doubt in Tony Davis' mind that Heaven is a city. During the moments he spent beyond the reality of this world, he recalls a vivid image:

> **TONY DAVIS**—These clouds opened up and through these clouds, I saw this huge city. It was so strange, but the city was beautiful.[115]

And Ricky Randolph, who barely survived injuries from a mountainside fall while hunting, says the city was "made up of what seemed to be glass or crystal."[116] Double pneumonia survivor George Ritchie describes the city as being "constructed out of light." He elaborates:

> **GEORGE RITCHIE**—At that time I had not read the book of Revelation, nor, incidentally, anything on the subject of life after death. But here was a city in which the walls, houses, streets seemed to give off light.[117]

The city's dimensions, as noted earlier, happen to be in the shape of a cube: they are described in the book of Revelation as having equal depth, width, and height. That unique shape is one of the things Boris Pilipshuk took in during his near-death experience:

> **BORIS PILIPSHUK**—In the center of [a] field stood a great city, in the form of a cube.

This city, the New Jerusalem, doesn't comprise the entire area of Heaven; it is its capital city. Massive in size, its base alone measures more than 200 million square miles. The walls around the New Jerusalem are described as having valuable gems as their foundation:

> The foundation stones of the city wall were adorned with every kind of precious stone. The first foundation stone was jasper; the second, sapphire; the third, chalcedony; the fourth, emerald; the fifth, sardonyx; the sixth, sardius; the seventh, chrysolite; the eighth, beryl; the ninth, topaz; the tenth, chrysoprase; the eleventh, jacinth; the twelfth, amethyst. (Revelation 21:19–20)

This list that looks like a jewelry store's inventory relates to one outstanding detail Betty Malz remembers seeing:

> **BETTY MALZ**—The wall to my right was higher now and made of many-colored, multi-tiered stones. A light from the other side of the wall shone through a long row of amber-colored gems several feet above my head. "Topaz," I thought to myself.[118]

In the walls that encircle the New Jerusalem stand twelve gates. And, yes, they are, in fact, "pearly." As it turns out, that common belief about Heaven isn't myth, but fact (see Revelation 21:21). With this in mind, consider what Darrel Young reports:

> **DARREL YOUNG**—I saw two sides of a beautiful walled city.… There was a gate in the wall leading off to the left side. Leading up to the gate was a staircase of magnificent beauty.… The gate was made of pearl, just as I expected, but I didn't expect it to be covered by diamonds, rubies, and other precious stones, with hinges of yellow gold.[119]

Malz glimpsed something similar. Accompanied by an angelic escort, she approached a gate that "was a solid sheet of pearl" that was "translucent so that I could almost, but not quite, see inside."[120]

The fact that the gates are made of pearl holds special meaning for those who have observed a stunning parallel:

> The fact is that these gates of pearl have a deep symbolic significance. A pearl speaks of beauty born out of pain. The beauty of a pearl comes from the pain of an oyster. A pearl is formed when a tiny grain of sand gets inside an oyster's shell, causing the oyster to become irritated and uncomfortable. The oyster relieves its pain by covering the irritating grain of sand with a soft, lustrous nacre that hardens into a beautiful, glowing pearl.

This is a beautiful picture of how the redeemed have emerged like a beautiful, luminous pearl out of the pain of Jesus Christ. The Lord told a story of just such a pearl. "The kingdom of heaven is like a merchant looking for fine pearls," He said. "When he found one of great value, he went away and sold everything he had and bought it" (Matthew 13:45–46). The merchant in the story is Jesus, who gave up everything—His prerogatives as God, the worship that is due Him, and even His mortal life—in order to redeem the saints, which He deemed a pearl of great price. He sold all He had to purchase you and me for Himself.[121]

Streets of Gold—Another snapshot we come to as we piece together a working sketch of our after-life destination features streets of gold: "And the street of the city was pure gold, as it were, transparent glass" (Revelation 21:18b, KJV). As it turns out, the streets of Jerusalem that had been littered with silver and gold during the peak years of King Solomon's reign served as just a small foreshadowing of what the streets of the New Jerusalem would be like.

BORIS PILIPSHUK—When I entered into the city through the gates, I stood in admiration. The city was made completely of gold. The gold was so pure—I had never seen such brilliance before. Gold streets, houses of gold, gold doors—everything was made of gold, transparent like glass.[122]

Natural Wonder—A third picture we can look at to get at least some idea of what Heaven is like features lush natural resources. Rather than being a return to the Garden of Eden, however (which, when you think about it, wouldn't be all that great because it would be "turning back the clock" on the progress made by people with God-given gifts, intellect, and creativity), it will be something more along the lines of "Eden, Part II"—or, as Randy Alcorn puts it, "Eden, only better."[123] He explains:

> Just like the Garden of Eden, the New Earth will be a place of sensory delight, breathtaking beauty, satisfying relationships, and personal joy. …In the same way that God paid attention to the details of the home he prepared for Adam and Eve in Eden, Christ is paying attention to the details as he prepares for us an eternal home in Heaven (John 14:2–3). If he prepared Eden so carefully and lavishly for mankind in the six days of creation, what has he fashioned in the place he's been preparing for us in the two thousand years since he left this world?[124]

Alcorn points out several passages of Scripture that refer to Heaven having "Eden-like qualities," including Isaiah 51:3, which describes the Lord making the wilderness like Eden, "and her desert like the garden of the Lord"; Ezekiel 36:35, which observes the "desolate land" becoming "like the garden of Eden"; Isaiah 35:1, speaking of the desert blossoming "as the rose"; and Isaiah 55:13, which describes a cypress tree replacing a thorn and a myrtle tree replacing the brier.

These lush natural wonders are a part of many personal near-death accounts. Betty Malz speaks of walking up a "beautiful green hill" that was blanketed with grass "the most vivid shade of green I had ever seen. Each blade was perhaps one inch long, the texture like fine velvet; every blade was vibrant and moving."[125]

And Richard Eby remembers the natural element of his peek into glory in great detail:

> **RICHARD EBY**—My gaze [was] riveted [by] the exquisite valley in which I found myself. Forests of symmetrical trees unlike anything on earth covered the foothills on each side. I could see each branch and "leaf"—not a brown spot or dead leaf in the forest.... Each tree, tall and graceful, was a duplicate of the others; perfect, unblemished.... The valley floor was gorgeous. Stately grasses, each blade perfect and erect, was interspersed with ultra-white, four-petaled flowers on stems two feet tall, with a touch of gold at the centers.[126]

Both of these descriptions are from people who took in these sights as part of some sort of valley surrounding the holy city. However, natural beauty is also a centerpiece of the city itself behind the bejeweled walls, with the river of life flowing directly from the throne of God as the source of nourishment (Revelation 22).

Jim Wilhelm caught a glimpse of such a river, which he described as deep and clear:

> **JIM WILHELM**—I was amazed that I could see right to the bottom of this beautiful river. The river was very deep. I was amazed at how clearly I could see the bright, shiny stones at the river's bottom. They looked like clear, shiny jewels.[127]

On the bank of the river of life, the Bible says, stands the Tree of Life. This isn't the same tree that got Adam and Eve into trouble; that's the Tree of the Knowledge of Good and Evil bearing the forbidden fruit (see Genesis 2:17). This is the tree that stood as a constant reminder to the first couple that eternal life would be the reward of an obedient life. As long as they followed God's single rule—"do not eat the fruit of the Tree of Knowledge of Good and Evil or you will surely die"—they were given full access to the Tree of Life. But since they broke that one rule, they were driven from the Garden, with God stationing an angelic guard with a flaming sword to bar the way to the Tree of Life, signifying that eternal life was no longer theirs. Just as they had been warned, they died, and through Adam's sin-tainted bloodline all generations to follow would die as well (see Romans 5:12). However, through salvation, mankind can be restored to the condition of complete perfection in the holy eyes of the Heavenly Father. When the physical body dies, believers will see and partake of the tree of life again in Heaven, where its breathtaking promise of eternal life is fulfilled.

Light—A final look at the characteristics of Heaven highlights something that's missing from what one would normally expect in a photograph of a hustling, bustling city: a light source. No sun gives light to the New Jerusalem by day; no moon comes out to illuminate the landscape at night. Neither are there streetlights, reading lamps, or night lights. That's because of the breathtaking truth that the Lord Himself is the perpetual Light of Heaven: "The greatest thing in Heaven is not the glory of the city itself," says John Hamby.[128] "Beyond the glory of the city itself, we have the Lamb who is the Light." This reality of God as the light source in Heaven is prophesied in Isaiah 60:1 and 19:

> Arise, shine; for your light has come, And the glory of the Lord has risen upon you.… No longer will you have the sun for light by day, Nor for brightness will the moon give you light; But you will have the Lord for an everlasting light, And your God for your glory. (Isaiah 60:1,19; see also Revelation 21:23)

Boris Pilipshuk's vision falls very much in line with this biblical truth. He describes seeing an "extraordinarily bright light at the center of the city" he entered during his near-death experience. Thinking back on the experience, he states:

BORIS PILIPSHUK—It was very interesting that I did not see a single shadow, not from the trees and not from the houses. There were no shadows, nor were there any lamps. I did not see the sun [or] any object that gave light, but the light was extraordinarily bright and so pleasant to the eyes. It was delightful beyond measure.[129]

Betty Malz also reports the puzzling phenomenon of seeing light with no visible source: "I saw no sun," she said, "but light was everywhere."[130]

Perhaps it's because of the purity of the light that *color* stands out so vividly in the recollections of many who have had brushes with eternity.

BUDDY FARRIS—As I looked, it seemed that a thousand rainbows were pouring out of that door. It was the most beautiful sight I have ever seen, with the most dazzling colours. With four children and fifty boxes of crayons around the house, I am familiar with colours! Attracted by the sight, I began walking towards it.[131]

JIM WILHELM—Everything we see on earth is dull in comparison to the colors that are in Heaven. All the colors were absolutely pure and very bright.[132]

A FOREVER HOME

"As a young child I can remember attempting to comprehend time without end…infinity. Now I realize that heaven is even beyond that which I failed to fathom as a child, for heaven is the end of time; in heaven there is no time at all."

Bob Deffinbaugh[133]

TERRY JAMES—I remember thinking: No! I don't want to leave. I never want to leave this wonderful place. The absolute peace had a gravity of its own, tugging me toward the throng, and I remember that the pull of the darkness in the opposite direction made the leaving emotionally draining. I wanted to stay forever, and yet everything again became dark, and I was thinking that I was having a nightmare.

I was in the land of my longing, where I had always wanted to be—where I belonged. This was a bad dream trying to take me from my home. Surely I soon would be back where I was safe, loved, and at peace. I would be back with those young people and the warm, inner glow would return.

Then the realization came into focus in my thinking. I wasn't having a bad dream that I was having a heart attack. This was the reality. I was back on the gurney, or the operating table of the cath lab.

Once you're home—especially after you've been away for a long time—it's hard to leave again. That's the not-so-great part of my otherwise spectacular near-death experience, and it's another facet shared by many others of their glimpses into glory. I simply did not want to leave that place. Jim Sepulveda describes having the same sensation after his heart attack. He states that after Christ expressed His love for him, and said, "But it is not your time yet. You must go back, for I have many works to do in you," Jim did not want to comply. "I stood in awe, unable to utter a sound," he recalls. "Within me I was protesting that I was never going back. I wanted to stay right there beside Him."[134]

Jim Wilhelm shared a similar reluctance to leave: "Then came the return trip through that same bright light," he says. "I did not want to return to earth, and kept asking that God please not send me back."[135]

Thankfully, there will come a time when we won't have to do that—ask the Lord to let us stay with Him. At that time, our move into our heavenly destination will be for a period of time that is so unlimited it's not even considered time. We'll finally be at home with our Lord...forever: "Surely goodness and lovingkindness will follow me all the days of my life, And I will dwell in the house of the Lord forever" (Psalm 23:6).

We cringe as we speak of spending an "eternity" in the waiting room of the doctor's office; we get downright dreamy-voiced when we say that we could sit on the beach with our toes in the sand "forever." Tossing around words that speak of infinity is something we do every day, yet "time without beginning or end"—which is what the words "eternity" and "infinity" mean— is one of the most difficult concepts we can ever try to grasp.

As tough as it can be to understand, a distinct sense of "eternity" is a striking facet common in many near-death experiences. In fact, Gerard Landry says it was his very first sensation after his heart stopped beating:

> **GERARD LANDRY**—The first awareness was of eternity. Like a watch, our body stops at that time. Yet our spirit and consciousness continue to live on in a dimension beyond sequential time.... I call it the eternal now, because that is how it felt to me. The past, present, and future are all merged into what Scripture calls eternity. Eternity is the present, the now that never ends.[136]

The Never-Ending "Now"

Theologically speaking, "the now that never ends," as Landry phrases it, is a great way to think of eternity and its perfect contrast to the "now that ends" here on Earth. The "now that ends," in fact, is what causes us some of the worst stress we ever experience as we push up against deadlines and wish that, somehow, some way, we could just "slow the hands of time." In Heaven, time will definitely be on our side, bringing us great "gain, not loss," says Randy Alcorn. He continues:

> The passing of time will no longer threaten us. It will bring new adventures without a sense of loss for what must end. We'll live with time, no longer under its pressure. When we see God face-to-face, time will pass, but we'll be lost in him.... Time will no longer be an hourglass in which the sands go from a limited past to a limited future. Our future will be unlimited. We'll no longer have to "number our days" (Psalm 90:12) or redeem the time, for time won't be a diminishing resource about to end.[137]

To many of us who behave much like the Disney version of Lewis Carroll's March Hare, who rushes around singing, "I'm late, I'm late," Heaven will be a welcome relief! In fact, Dr. Richard Eby says that during his experience, "Instantly, the sense of timelessness made all hurry foolish."[138]

The fact that time will not be our enemy in Heaven is enough to launch any heart into deep longing for that heavenly home. But even that fabulous fact will be overshadowed by the breathtaking reality of who it is we'll be spending eternity with:

El Olam, the everlasting God, "our dwelling place in all generations" (Psalm 90:1).

"When our bodies die," says John Piper, "we do not experience any break in our fellowship with God through Christ. Our fellowship, in fact, in that instant is perfected (Hebrews 12:23). The life we have with Christ in God today, because of the new birth, will never end. We will not see the end of it. And we will not taste the end of it. Because there is no end of it."[139]

Chapter Seven

HOPE!

"I do not want you to be ignorant, brethren, concerning those who have fallen asleep, lest you sorrow as others who have no hope" (1 Thessalonians 4:13).

"The fear of hell and eternal torment may be a strong incentive for salvation…but it is not the basis for our hope and faith. In the Bible heaven is the ground of our faith and hope."

Bob Deffinbaugh[140]

Through Jesus' words and the accounts from those who have been given previews of Heaven and/or Hell, we've been able to put together a spectacular (although far from complete) montage of Heaven's glories as well as an all-too-vivid snapshot of Hell's horrors. By comparison, even the smallest glimpse of Hell makes the worst parts of our world seem like Heaven, doesn't it?

But in truth, as we've already discussed, where we live now is far from being the perfect environment it was originally designed to be. And if you think the troubles of life seem to be getting worse, you're right. Biblical prophecy has long foretold some of the things that would face us as the end of this world's history approaches. Take some time and read through the predictions found in Matthew 24:1–14 and 2 Timothy 3:1–5. You'll find lists that sound all too familiar as we look around. Whether in the arena of nature, politics, family relationships, or spiritual matters, humanity seems to be confronted with huge problems that need to be tunneled through. For many, it's a seemingly hopeless situation.

Consider the bleak definition of hopelessness: "Having no expectation of good or success."[141] Too many people today wake up each morning to live out these words as truth. They find themselves with no expectations of either good or success, and that's a dark place to be. It's such a dark place, in fact, that those in the medical field cite a strong connection between hopelessness and physical, emotional, and mental illnesses.

The good news is that there is hope. For anyone who chooses to trust Christ as Savior, "hope" is not a word in the language of therapeutic psychobabble or positivity talk; it's truth solidly centered on the reality of the Word of God.

Hope-Giving Promises

"Let us hold fast the confession of our hope without wavering, for He who promised is faithful" (Hebrews 10:23).

By some counts, there are anywhere from three thousand to eight thousand "precious and magnificent" promises of good things in the Bible.[142] The number of promises isn't nearly as important as their content. Assurances ranging from God's help with our problems to His constant presence when we're lonely often serve as our only steady foothold when we're hiking across rocky ground.

Some of the greatest promises we find in God's Word have to do with Heaven and the lives we can look forward to living even after our physical bodies die. Hopelessness can cause depression, apathy, and lethargy, making it difficult to even throw one foot over the side of the bed in the morning. On the other hand, hopefulness—fueled by the prospects of a bright future—not only helps us get both feet on the floor, but it helps us get dressed, put on our shoes, and keep putting one foot in front of another all day long, every day. When the challenges and trials of daily life threaten to knock us back off of our feet, the writer of Hebrews encourages us to "hold fast" to hope because it's such a valuable commodity!

Practically speaking, holding fast to hope—specifically, the hope of Heaven—while we're walking the sidewalks and corridors of this Earth offers lots of perks. Here are just a few:

1. *The hope of Heaven motivates us to live for Christ.* While we're busy bringing home the bacon in an effort to shore up our savings accounts, thoughts of Heaven keep us focused on the more important endeavor: storing up treasures that have eternal value. As we talked about in chapter 4, what we do for Christ while we're alive has a direct link to the rewards we'll be able to lay at His feet in Heaven.

2. *The hope of Heaven takes the edge off of the sadness that comes after believers we love die.* Losing a loved one is painful for anyone. But experiencing the death of a loved one who was a follower of Christ is a shorter-lived sorrow. "For the unbeliever who has no hope, no faith-certainty, death is crushing, exceedingly sorrowful," says author Paige Patterson. However, "the believer sorrows some over the momentary separation, but he does not sorrow as those who have no hope. Death for a believer is just…a limited and, on the time-scale of eternity, brief dislocation."[143]

3. *The hope of Heaven gives us perspective.* When thinking of eternity and the breathtaking promises Heaven has in store, none of our worldly problems—whether as small

as a computer crash or as large as a national disaster—seem so insurmountable.

4. *The hope of Heaven gives us joy.* The truth is, many of us spend far more time and energy researching our vacation destinations than we do our heavenly destination. If the Lord found Heaven an important enough place in which to build His bride, the church, eternal dwellings (John 14:1–3), and to include mention of that heavenly city more than five hundred times in Scripture, shouldn't we consider it a heavenly imperative, urging us to give it some serious thought? The stunning details He provides about Heaven should cause us to practically jump up and down with excitement! (See for yourself: Check out Revelation 4, or 19, or 21, for starters.)

5. *The hope of Heaven is a great segue way into sharing the truth of God's love.* Many people in the world today are without hope—and they don't even know what they're missing. As believers who harbor hope in our hearts, evidence of that hope is bound to come tumbling out of our mouths or be seen in our actions from time to time. Chances are our hope-filled words or actions will generate some questions from those around us. Further, Heaven and things having to do with life after death are intriguing topics—virtually everyone is curious about the possibilities. For those very reasons and others, we're instructed to "always be ready to make a defense to everyone who asks you to give an account for the hope that is in you" (1 Peter 3:15). The more we

know about Heaven, the more we can share the wonderful things that God has "prepared for those who love Him" (1 Corinthians 2:9).

6. *The hope of Heaven is imminent.* We know our days are numbered. We also know that on the biblical timeline of end-time events (see appendix B), nothing is left to take place before the Rapture of the church. So either way—whether by death or by the sounding of the trumpet of 1 Corinthians 15:52—the hope of Heaven is closer than we might think. As a matter of fact, Christ's any-moment return for us in the Rapture is God's great promise to keep us from the time of His wrath that must come upon this sin-fallen Earth. We're told to comfort each other with this promise (1 Thessalonians 5:11).

The Blessed Hope!

Certainly when my heart stopped beating on that Good Friday, my condition appeared hopeless. Those caring for me had no reason to expect that I would survive a type of heart attack that kills 90 to 95 percent of its victims. Neither did the situation appear anything but hopeless for Buddy Farris after he was "slapped like a pinball between the vehicles" and injured so badly at the scene of an accident that the rescue squad covered his face with a sheet after spending thirty minutes trying to resuscitate him.[144] We could say the same about virtually everyone whose near-death experience we've looked at in these pages: "Near death" appears to be a hopeless condition. But the Bible assures us that as long as we have life, we have hope (see Ecclesiastes 9:4).

Because I had made the decision to place my trust in Christ as a child of six years of age, I enjoyed that hope even as I was on the brink of death. In fact, not once did I have any anxiety whatsoever that I might die. It just never crossed my mind.

Jesus was with me—and is with me to this writing. He sent the Holy Spirit to indwell me, to live in the hearts of all believers, once He ascended to the Father's throne in our future home, Heaven: "But when the Comforter is come, whom I will send unto you from the Father, even the Spirit of truth, which proceedeth from the Father, he shall testify of me" (John 15:26, KJV). The testimony of Jesus is the spirit of prophecy, according to Revelation 9:10. That testimony is one of supreme hope, no matter how troubling or frightening our times and circumstances.

According to the apostle Paul in Titus 2: 13, Jesus is the "blessed hope!"

HeavenVision Unveiled
By Terry James

There are no coincidences in God's dealings with His children. So it was that He has dealt with me through the clinical death I experienced Good Friday, April 22, 2011. I lived through that ordeal and am here now, writing about it for purposes He has determined. He has shown me, without the slightest doubt in my spirit and mind, exactly what my near-death experiences meant. Therefore, without any reservation, I am putting down for the record the message I know my Father in Heaven wants me to deliver at this time.

I write these things with a profound sense of humility, however. I am nobody special, other than a child of God through the shed blood of my Savior and Lord, Jesus Christ.

WHEN HEAVEN AND EARTH
INTERSECTED FOR ME

Near the end of the year 2010, two projects came into my thoughts. The first was for a series of articles for our www.rap-tureready.com website and the second was, as stated earlier in this book, the book on Heaven my mother and her sister wanted me to write.

I began writing the website series, which I called "Scanning a Fearful Future," for Rapture Ready's weekly "Nearing Midnight" column. The last of the ten articles was posted January 24, 2011. One of the primary reasons I wanted to write the series was to try to help provide answers from the prophetic Word because so many who visit the website were concerned about where the national and worldwide economic upheaval was leading. Also, Rapture Ready's founder, Todd Strandberg, and I were getting an increasing number of emails accusing us of being heretics who were leading people to Hell with our pretribulational teaching. We believe the Bible teaches that Christ will come for His followers in the Rapture *before*, not during or after, the seven-year period of Tribulation.

"Christians should be prepared to face the coming Tribulation and Antichrist," we were told in scathing rants. By not preparing Christians to face the beast described in Revelation 13, they said, they wouldn't know to reject Antichrist's mark and number. As a matter of fact, we were already *in* the Tribulation, many of the emailers were telling us.

Along with those two projects going through my mind were persistent prayer requests: *Lord, I know what your Word says. The pretribulation view of the Rapture is the correct one, I believe. But, please give me your unmistakable confirmation of this Truth. We don't want to lead people astray.* I also asked the Lord for affirmation in my spirit that what I believe He gave me to write, I had faithfully written.

So when I clinically died not once, but three times—on Good Friday, no less—what I experienced was the Lord making a statement, I'm absolutely convinced in the deepest reaches of my spirit. The first thought to penetrate my realization while lying in the hospital bed was that the beautiful, joyful, cheering young people who greeted me each time my heart stopped was—and is— the "cloud of witnesses" described in Hebrews 12:1–3. The second thing that pierced my spiritual understanding several days later was that the cheering they greeted me with in that heavenly setting was approval of my writing about and teaching about Bible prophecy.

It was burned deeply into my understanding that all of this cheering was affirmation from the Heavenly Father not just for me, but for all of His children who believe and teach about Bible prophecy in these last of the last days before His Son calls His church to Himself (Revelation 4:1), as He promised in John 14:1–3.

Later, over the weeks and months of recuperation, I've been given even deeper understanding of those glimpses into glory. My series of articles is key to the "HeavenVision" the Lord continues to impress upon me. The articles were begun to help allay the fears that were coming to my inbox fast and furiously around the time when the economic collapse of America and the world seemed imminent.

The question that was in every email on the topic of the "coming economic collapse" was based upon a well-known TV pundit's declaration that Americans could awaken on any morning and find that the world had changed completely. The U.S. dollar would be no longer of any value. Worldwide depression would quickly bring changes that would in its course bring martial law and imprisonment for all who didn't toe the mark of what Big Brother demanded.

Most notes at the time expressed fear that Christians in America would be put in Federal Emergency Management Agency (FEMA) internment camps—which were said to be popping up all around the country, according to many blogs and conspiracy theory-laden websites.

Would Christians in America face martyrdom—and maybe even have to face the Antichrist regime? Maybe the pretribulational Rapture view wasn't prophetic truth after all. Maybe we already *were* in the Tribulation!

The series covered ten weeks, so there isn't room in this book to put all that was presented in it. However, the bottom line in answer to the fear-filled emails was and is the following conclusion.

Jesus Provides Answer

The series of articles brought me, in the final analysis, to the words of the greatest of all prophets —the Lord Jesus Christ.

> And as it was in the days of Noe, so shall it be also in the days of the Son of man. They did eat, they drank, they married wives, they were given in marriage, until the day that Noe entered into the ark, and the flood came, and destroyed them all. Likewise also as it was in the days of Lot; they did eat, they drank, they bought, they sold, they planted, they builded; But the same day that Lot went out of Sodom it rained fire and brimstone from heaven, and destroyed them all. Even thus shall it be in the day when the Son of man is revealed. (Luke 17:26–30, KJV)

Another Gospel account expounds further upon Jesus' prophecy about conditions that will prevail at the moment He next intervenes into human history.

> But of that day and hour knoweth no man, no, not the angels of heaven, but my Father only. But as the days of Noe were, so shall also the coming of the Son of

man be. For as in the days that were before the flood
they were eating and drinking, marrying and giving in
marriage, until the day that Noe entered into the ark,
And knew not until the flood came, and took them all
away; so shall also the coming of the Son of man be.
Then shall two be in the field; the one shall be tak-
en, and the other left. Two women shall be grinding
at the mill; the one shall be taken, and the other left.
Watch therefore: for ye know not what hour your Lord
doth come. (Matthew 24:36–42, KJV)

The conclusion reached in the series—based upon the above
prophecy by Jesus—was that there will be no catastrophic man-
made or natural event that will throw the nation and world suddenly into the time of apocalyptic chaos. It will be Christ's sud-
den call to His church that will bring on God's judgment.

It will be "business as usual," with people buying, selling, building, marrying, etc., right up until the moment when born-again
believers instantaneously go to be with their Lord when He calls
them in the Rapture.

Jesus couldn't have been prophesying about the time of His
Second Advent (Revelation 19:11). At the time He returns, when
the battle of Armageddon is raging in the valley of Megiddo, it
will not be business as usual (see Luke 17: 26–30 and Matthew
24:36–42). At the time of that great battle, as many as two-thirds
of humanity will have been killed by the events of the Tribulation
era (the last seven years of human history before Christ's Second
Coming). There's nothing everyday or routine about that.

I have had confirmed in my spirit through the cheering of the "cloud of witnesses" that what I wrote is the way things will unfold. The Lord of Heaven, Himself, is preventing the total collapse of the world economic system, as He is keeping all-out war from breaking out in the Middle East.

When Christ steps out on the clouds of glory and shouts: "Come up here!" (Revelation 4:1), judgment will begin to fall upon America and the world that very day.

HEAVENVISION AFTERTHOUGHTS...

Not long after Angie and I began researching and writing this book, I was engrossed in listening to a television program. I don't remember what it was about; it was probably a ball game of some sort. Seemingly out of nowhere, I heard an inner voice speak, almost audibly.

"Terry, you remember praying all of those months, before the Good Friday experience, asking to have confirmed in your spirit that the pretrib view of the Rapture is the absolute Truth from my Word? Well...what do you think that cheering group of youngsters was all about?"

It was all I could do to keep myself from leaping through the ceiling from my sitting position! The epiphany was stunning! And the next moment brought the humbling realization that the Lord of all creation would be so loving as to spend such an intimate moment with someone like me.

I was being cheered for teaching, specifically, the pretrib Rapture view. This assured me that the pretrib Rapture is the true meaning of the apostle Paul's prophetic writing to the Corinthians in 1 Corinthians 15:51–55 and to the Thessalonians in 1 Thessalonians 4:13–18. Again came the prompting in my spirit that the cheering wasn't for me alone, but for all who hold to and teach and preach this view in these final hours of the age.

Some time before that, another Holy Spirit epiphany had illuminated my spiritual understanding of my Good Friday visit to what I believe must have been somewhere near the portals of Heaven.

While I was standing before that group of people each time my heart stopped beating, one face stood out from among the rest. Her smile was wide, her face beaming with joy, while she was thrusting her arms upward as if celebrating victory at a sports event. On the third and last visit to that otherworldly place of stunning beauty and absolute peace, the young woman looked over at me while we were all running as if in a race, her hands raised in victory. She was laughing, her beautiful facial expression bursting with unbridled exultation.

That face was constantly with me for more than a month following my trip to that realm. Her image never left my conscious thoughts until her identity emerged suddenly into my mind at a rare moment when I wasn't thinking about it.

While the last vestiges of my eyesight had been in the process of fading to darkness, I had begun my first book that focused on Bible prophecy. I called it *Storming toward Armageddon*. During that time, I became friends with an elderly woman who could no longer attend our church because she had reached the advanced stages of osteoporosis.

She was a great Christian lady who loved Bible prophecy, and she also was a very good poet. Many of her poems involved biblical prophecy, as a matter of fact. Additionally, she taught several classes of young women each week in her home. They would sit on the floor surrounding her while she taught the Bible studies.

We talked regularly by phone, and I visited her from time to time. She was excited about the fact that I was about to become an author of a book about prophecy. I asked her if we could use one of her brief poems in that book. She readily agreed, and we put the poem at the beginning of that book. We also put her poems in my next two books, and she lived to see them in print.

My friend began to lose her ability to see, so we commiserated over our mutual eye problems. Her health declined quickly, and she died before she lost her eyesight totally.

The Lord has confirmed in the deepest reaches of my spirit that the dynamic, joyfully cheering young woman of my visit to the outskirts of glory, whose beautiful face continues to be etched in my mind's eye, is Arbra Carman—this wonderful friend and Christian sister.

Strange winds whisper sounds of storm;

Judgment may fall soon.

Awake, brother, sister, awake!

I see a harvest moon.

–Arbra Carman

APPENDIX A

TERRY'S THANK YOUS

Terry wishes to thank the medical team who provided his care during his heart attack, hospitalization, and recovery:

Emergency Responders: Ray Lewis, paramedic; Craig Hicks, EMT

Saline Memorial Hospital Emergency Department: Regina Bennett, RN; Justin White, Emergency Department MD

Saline Memorial Hospital Cath Lab: Eric Bain, RN; JoAnn Heinz, cardiovascular technician/clinical coordinator; Dr. Aravind Rao Nemarkommula, "Dr. Rao," interventional cardiologist

Saline Memorial Hospital Critical Care: Dr. Alan Hatch, cardiologist; Lori Fite, RN; Kelly Tucker, RN; Michael Bush, RN; Ashley Fleming, RN; and Virginia Strickland, RN

Saline Heart Group: Zack Hyatt, exercise physiologist; Amber Prins, registered dietitian

APPENDIX B

SEQUENCE OF LIFE-AFTER-LIFE EVENTS

While the theology of Heaven and doctrine concerning the afterlife can seem overly complex, the sequence of events once we die is really quite straightforward according to God's Word.

First comes physical death (if the Rapture doesn't happen first). When we die, if we have chosen to follow Christ, our souls immediately leave the body to enter this intermediate state. That is where our souls will remain—in that "present Heaven" with, most agree, some type of a temporary, clothed, heavenly body —until the Rapture of the Church. That is the time described in 1 Thessalonians 4:16–17, when:

> The Lord Himself will descend from heaven with a shout, with the voice of the archangel and with the trumpet of God, and the dead in Christ will rise first. Then we who are alive and remain will be caught up together with them in the clouds to meet the Lord in the air, and so we shall always be with the Lord.

At that moment, the flesh-and-blood bodies of all who are still alive on Earth will be changed into supernatural bodies—transformed into the likeness of Christ's glorified body (we are told that our mortal flesh can't inherit the heavenly Kingdom; see 1 Corinthians 15:50). At that instant, all who have died to that point in history will have their temporary, heavenly forms joined to their supernaturally transformed bodies in which they lived while on Earth.

All of these believers of the Church Age (the Age of Grace), then, will be with the Lord in Heaven, while on Earth, the terrible time described as the Great Tribulation will be underway. At the conclusion of that seven-year period, which will reach its climax at the battle of Armageddon, Christ will return with His saints to the earth to put an end to that last great battle of the age, the final war between the armies of Christ and of Satan. This is known as Christ's Second Coming or Second Advent. That's when He will establish His thousand-year reign, or millennial reign, on Earth (referenced in Revelation 19:11).

When Jesus comes back at that time, all saints of all the ages—including believers both before and after Christ's death, burial, and resurrection, will be resurrected to life. (The Old Testament believers will have also been in temporary, heavenly bodies.) They will be joined to their supernaturally transformed earthly bodies at this time.

All who survived the terrible seven years of Tribulation immediately leading up to Christ's Second Advent will be judged by Christ in the "sheep and goats judgment of nations" described in Matthew 25. After the millennial reign of the Lord Jesus Christ has run its course, the heavens and Earth will be completely re-made.

But before that, the Great White Throne Judgment will take place, with all the lost souls of all of human history being judged by Christ. These rebels against God will be cast into the lake of fire, the place which was originally prepared for Satan and all of the angelic hordes who rebelled against God when Lucifer de-termined to put himself above God (see Isaiah 14:14).

ENDNOTES

1   Billy Graham. *The Journey* (Nashville, TN: Zondervan, 2006), 298.

2   Mark Hitchcock, *55 Answers to Questions about Life after Death* (Sisters, OR: Multnomah, 2005), 55.

3   May, 1827.

4   C. S. Lewis, "To Mary Willis Shelburne," *Collected Letters* (June 28, 1963).

5   III, i, 65–68.

6   See also Daniel 12:2; 1 Corinthians 15:20, 51; and 1 Thessalonians 4:14.

7   John MacArthur, *The Glory of Heaven: The Truth about Heaven, Angels and Eternal Life* (Wheaton, IL: Crossway, 1996), 71.

8   Lori Victa and Kathy Chiero, "Don Piper: At Heaven's Gate," CBN.com, http://www.cbn.com/700club/features/amazing/donpiper_heaven051104.aspx.

9   MacArthur, 76.

10   Randy Alcorn, *Heaven* (Carol Stream, IL: Tyndale House, 2004), 41–42.

11   For an overview of the sequence of after-life events as described in the Bible, see appendix B.

12   Wayne Grudem, *Systematic Theology* (Grand Rapids, MI: Zondervan, 1994), 820.

13   "Officer Resurrected: An Interview with Boris Pilipshuk," FreeCDTracts.com, http://www.freecdtracts.com/testimony/boris_pilipchuk.htm.

14   Rita Bennett, *To Heaven and Back* (Grand Rapids, MI: Zondervan, 1997).

15   Alcorn, 47.

16   Darrel Young "The Story of Darrel Young," freechristianteaching.org, http://www.freechristianteaching.org/modules/smartsection/item.php?itemid=261#axzz26ftRD2Xc.

17   Richard Wright, "The Story of Richard Wright," freechristianteaching.org, http://www.freechristianteaching.org/modules/smartsection/item.php?itemid=259#axzz26ftRD2Xc.

18   Victa and Chiero.

19   W. A. Criswell and Paige Patterson, *Heaven* (Wheaton, IL: Living Books,1991), 30.

20   Hitchcock, 170.

21   Lehman Strauss, "Shall We Know Each Other in Heaven?" Bible.org, http://bible.org/seriespage/shall-we-know-each-other-heaven.

22   John MacArthur, "Biography," One Place, http://www.oneplace.com/ministries/turning-point/read/articles/biography-12377.html.

23   Randy Alcorn, "Will We Desire Relationships in Heaven?" Eternal Perspective Ministries, 4/26/10, http://www.epm.org/resources/2010/Apr/26/will-we-desire-relationships-heaven/.

24   Hitchcock, 229.

25   Bob Glaze, *Angels: A Historical and Prophetic Study* (Oklahoma City: Hearthstone, 1998), 58.

26   That's why the writer of Hebrews urges us not to "forget to entertain strangers, for by so doing some have unwittingly entertained angels," reinforcing the idea that in our mortal bodies, we usually won't recognize the heavenly beings when we encounter them (see Hebrews 13:20).

27   Joni Eareckson Tada, *Heaven: Your Real Home* (Grand Rapids, MI: Zondervan, 1995), 83. Note: Joni Eareckson Tada is a Christian author, artist, and speaker who has been a paraplegic since a diving accident in 1967 left her paralyzed from the shoulders down.

28   Royston Fraser, "The Story of Royston Fraser," freechristianteaching.org, http://www.freechristianteaching.org/modules/smartsection/item.php?itemid=232#axzz26ftRD2Xc.

29   Gerard Sybers, "Don't Despair. God Is in Love with His People," freecdtracts.com, http://www.freecdtracts.com/testimony/gerard_sybers.htm.

30   Betty Malz, "My Glimpse of Eternity," near-death.com, http://www.near-death.com/forum/nde/000/85.html.

31   Billy Graham, *Angels* (Waco, TX: Word, 1986), 117.

32   Hitchcock, 163.

33   One important note before leaving the topic of angels: A common human response to death involves the idea that we somehow transform into angels when we die. "Heaven has gained a new angel" is a refrain heard often among many people who are trying to comfort the recently bereaved. However, this is contrary to what the Bible says about our death and angels. Scripture makes it plain that we will not *turn into angels*; but we will be in their presence. They are not worthy of our worship. (Perhaps the Lord has withheld the details because He knows we would have a tendency to worship them if we knew the truth about their power, appearance, and actions!)

34   Alcorn, *Heaven,* 171.

35   Ron Rhodes, *The Wonder of Heaven: A Biblical Tour of Our Eternal Home* (Eugene, OR: Harvest House, 2009), 29.

36   "Heaven and Hell: Dr. George Ritchie's Near-Death Experience," near-death.com, http://www.near-death.com/ritchie.html.

37   Sybers.

38   Young.

39   Richard L. Strauss, "God is Love," Bible.org, http://bible.org/seriespage/god-love.

40   Harold W. Hohner, "Ephesians," Bible Knowledge Commentary: New Testament (Colorado Springs, CO: Victor, 2004), 623–624.

41   Rhodes, 147.

42   Beth Moore, *John: the Beloved Disciple Student Edition* (Trust Media, 2003), 110.

43   Tada, 39.

44   Hitchcock, 209–209. This list is abbreviated.

45   Graham, *Journey*, 304.

46   Grudem, 831.

47   Richard Eby, "The Sights of Paradise," an excerpt from *A Physician's Amazing Account of Being 'Caught Up into Paradise*,' bibleprobe.com, http://www.bibleprobe.com/dreby.htm.

48   Malz.

49   Paul Kusiak, "What Heaven Will Be Like," Rapture Ready, http://raptureready.com/soap/heaven.html.

50   Alcorn, *Heaven*, 57.

51   Eby.

52   MacArthur, 222.

53   Grudem, 749.

54   Paul Harnett, "What's in a Name?" Jesus-Resurrection.info, http://www.jesus-resurrection.info/whats-in-name.html.

55   Ritchie.

56   Ricky Randolph, "Witness to a Miracle," near-death.com, http://near-death.com/randolph.html.

57   Bennett.

58   Charles Stanley, "How God Reveals His Will," InTouch.org, http://www.intouch.org/resources/bible-studies/content/topic/how_god_reveals_his_will_study.

59   Rod Thomas, "Tony Davis: Unfinished Business on Earth," CBN.com, http://www.cbn.
      com/700club/features/amazing/Tony_Davis_050908.aspx.

60   Jim Sepulveda, "The Story of Jim Sepulveda, USA," freechristianteaching.org, http://www.
      freechristianteaching.org/modules/smartsection/item.php?itemid=218#axzz1dgyTD1sj.

61   Simon Mackrell, "The Story of Simon Mackrell," freechristianteaching.org, http://www.
      freechristianteaching.org/modules/smartsection/item.php?com_mode=thread&com_or
      der=0&itemid=268#axzz26ftRD2Xc.

62   Tada, 204

63   Christine Eastell, "The Story of Christine Eastell, UK," freechristianteaching.org, http://www.
      freechristianteaching.org/modules/smartsection/item.php?itemid=227#axzz1vejpN7Wv.

64   Charles Honey, "Belief in Hell Dips, But Some Say They've Already Been There," The Pew
      Forum on Religion and Public Life, 8/14/08, http://www.pewforum.org/Religion-News/
      Belief-in-hell-dips-but-some-say-theyve-already-been-there.aspx.

65   Don Whitaker, "Divine Revelations: Face to Face Encounters with Jesus Christ,"
      spiritlessons.com, .http://spiritlessons.com/documents/Rawlings/Dr_Rawlings_Near_
      Death_Experiences.htm.

66   That's simply not true, of course, because: 1) Heaven will be as far from boring as we can
      imagine, and 2) Isolation is one of the many torments Hell's inhabitants will experience for
      eternity.

67   Gary Stearman, Time Travelers of the Bible (Crane, MO: Defender, 2011), 163.

68   C.S. Lewis, The Problem of Pain (New York: Macmillan, 1962), 118.

69   John Piper, "The Present Power of Heaven and Hell," Desiring God.org, 4/27/94, http://
      www.desiringgod.org/resource-library/taste-see-articles/the-present-power-of-heaven-
      and-hell.

70   Tommy Clayton, "The Severity of Hell," Grace to You, 5/11/11, http://www.gty.org/blog/
      B110511.

71   Ronald Reagan, "Divine Revelations: Face to Face Encounters with Jesus Christ,"
      spiritlessons.com, http://spiritlessons.com/documents/Rawlings/Dr_Rawlings_Near_
      Death_Experiences.htm.

72   Angie Fenimore, "Angie Fenimore's NDE," an excerpt from Beyond the Darkness: My Near-
      Death Journey to the Edge of Hell and Back, bibleprobe.com, http://www.bibleprobe.com/
      angiefenimore.htm.

73   Clayton.

74   Fenimore.

75   Louis A. Barbieri, Jr., "Matthew," Bible Knowledge Commentary (Colorado Springs, CO: Victor,
      2004), 50.

76   Eastell.

77   Joe T. Horn, "Five Myths about Hell," JoeTHorn.net, 8/10/10, http://www.joethorn. net/2010/08/10/five-myths-about-hell-2/.

78   John MacArthur, "A Testimony of One Surprised to Be in Hell, Part 2," Grace to You, 4/30/06, http://www.gty.org/resources/sermons/42-213.

79   Mickey Robinson, "The Story of Mickey Robinson," freechristianteaching.org, http://www. freechristianteaching.org/modules/smartsection/item.php?itemid=245#axzz1vns9rwp2. Emphasis added.

80   Alcorn, Heaven, 23.

81   John MacArthur, "Saved or Self-Deceived, Part 2" Grace to You, 11/11/07, http://www.gty. org/Resources/Sermons/80-327.

82   Robinson

83   Reagan.

84   Reagan.

85   2 Thessalonians 1:9; Clayton, "Severity of Hell."

86   Graham, Journey, 299.

87   Mackrell.

88   Pilipshuk.

89   Angie Peters, Life of David (Nashville, TN: Thomas Nelson, 2008), 4.

90   Ibid.

91   Larry Richards, The Bible (Nashville, TN: Thomas Nelson, 1998), 8.

92   Ibid., 7.

93   Jim Palmer, Divine Nobodies: Shedding Religion to Find God (Nashville, TN: W Publishing, 2006), 185.

94   Ruth Bell Graham, Footprints of a Pilgrim (Nashville, TN: Word, 2001), 36.

95   D. A. Carson, Basics for Believers: An Exposition of Philippians (Grand Rapids: Baker, 1996), 93.

96   Jim Wilhelm, "Jim Wilhelm's Heaven Testimony," freecdtracts.com, http://www.freecdtracts. com/testimony/JimWilhelm.htm.

97   David Guzik, "David Guzik's Commentaries on the Bible," studylight.org, http://www. studylight.org/com/guz/view.cgi?book=re&chapter=21&verse=12#Re21_12).

98   Anne Graham Lotz, "Billy Graham's Daughter: Here Are Eight Secrets about Heaven You Didn't Know!" Beliefnet.com, http://www.beliefnet.com/Entertainment/Galleries/Billy-Grahams-daughter-secrets-about-heaven.aspx?p=4#ixzz1uyFaadls.

99   United States Census Bureau, "Current Population Clock," 9/9/12, http://www.census.gov/main/www/popclock.html.

100 This is a 2012 estimate. "Population Growth Rate," Central Intelligence Agency, https://www.cia.gov/library/publications/the-world-factbook/fields/2002.html.

101 Rhodes, 121–122.

102 Alexander Maclaren, "The Rest of Faith," from Alexander Maclaren Sermons on the Epistle to the Hebrews, Part 2, PreceptAustin.org, http://www.preceptaustin.org/maclaren_on_hebrews_pt2.htm#eigr.

103 Bob Deffinbaugh, "A Heaven to Seek," Bible.org, http://bible.org/seriespage/heaven-seek-revelation-211-225.

104 Michael Vlach, "Man Created to Rule Over God's Creation," TheologicalStudies.org, 6/22/11, http://theologicalstudies.org/blog/412-man-created-to-rule-over-gods-creation.

105 Grudem, 1161. (See also Daniel 7:27 and Luke 19:16–17).

106 David Jeremiah, Worship (Atlanta: Walk Thru the Bible Ministries, 1995), 7.

107 Ibid., 69.

108 Ibid., 71.

109 Malz.

110 Eby.

111 Criswell, 14.

112 Criswell, 188.

113 Charles Spurgeon, "Rest," Sermon 866, delivered 4/18/1869, SpurgeonGems.org, http://www.spurgeongems.org/vols13-15/chs866.pdf.

114 Maclaren.

115 Davis.

116 Randolph.

117 Ritchie.

118 Malz.

119 Young.

120 Malz.

121 Lambert Dolphin, "Jerusalem Above, Jerusalem Below," LDolphin.org, http://www. ldolphin.org/jerusabove.html.

122 Pilipshuk.

123 Alcorn, *Heaven*, 244.

124 Ibid., 241–242.

125 Malz.

126 Eby.

127 Wilhelm.

128 John Hamby, "Life in the Heavenly City," SermonCentral.com, http://www.sermoncentral. com/sermons/life-in-the-heavenly-city-john-hamby-sermon-on-heaven-92275. asp?page=3.

129 Pilipshuk.

130 Malz.

131 Buddy Farris, "The Story of Buddy Farris," freechristianteaching.org, http://www. freechristianteaching.org/modules/smartsection/item.php?itemid=247#axzz1dgyTD1sj.

132 Wilhelm.

133 Deffinbaugh.

134 Sepulveda.

135 Wilhelm.

136 Landry.

137 Alcorn, *Heaven*, 269.

138 Eby.

139 John Piper, "You Will Never See Death," Preachitteachit.org, http://bible.org/seriespage/ heaven-seek-revelation-211-225.

140 Deffinbaugh.

141 Merriam-Webster.com.

142 2 Peter 1:4.

143 Criswell and Patterson, 222.

144 Farris.